QUOTES to Inspire Great Reading Teachers

A Reflective Tool for Advancing Students' Literacy

Cathy Collins Block   Susan E. Israel

CORWIN PRESS
A SAGE Publications Company
Thousand Oaks, California

KH

For information:

Corwin Press
A Sage Publications Company
2455 Teller Road
Thousand Oaks, California 91320
www.corwinpress.com

Sage Publications Ltd.
1 Oliver's Yard
55 City Road
London EC1Y 1SP
United Kingdom

Sage Publications India Pvt. Ltd.
B-42, Panchsheel Enclave
Post Box 4109
New Delhi 110 017 India

Printed in the United States of America

Library of Congress Cataloging-in-Publication Data

Block, Cathy Collins.
Quotes to inspire great reading teachers: A reflective tool for advancing students' literacy / Cathy Collins Block, Susan E. Israel.
    p. cm.
Includes bibliographical references (p.) and index.
ISBN 1-4129-2647-5 (cloth) — ISBN 1-4129-2648-3 (pbk.)
   1. Reading—Aids and devices. 2. Quotations, English. I. Israel, Susan E. II. Title.
LB1573.39.B57 2006
372.4—dc22

                                           2006002315

This book is printed on acid-free paper.

06 07 08 09 10   10 9 8 7 6 5 4 3 2 1

Acquisitions Editor:	Jean Ward
Editorial Assistant:	Jordan Barbakow
Production Editor:	Melanie Birdsall
Typesetter:	C&M Digitals (P) Ltd.
Copyeditor:	Cate Huisman
Indexer:	Sheila Bodell
Cover Designer:	Scott Van Atta

6/23/06

Contents

Reflections From the Authors

I first realized the power of using quotes when I began teaching. I used to write the quotes on the board and students began asking me questions about their meaning. I realized using quotes can be a powerful tool to deepen critical thinking about a topic. My first three books on quotes were published by the School of Education at Texas Christian University. Quotes can be used to begin the learning day and extend it beyond the day's close.

—Cathy Collins Block, PhD, Professor,
Texas Christian University

I have always enjoyed reading an inspirational quote that helped me think differently about something or extend my thinking beyond the obvious. I enjoy using quotes in my teaching as a professor by placing them on my syllabus, assignments, and assessment measures. I also like to place inspirational quotes on the chalkboard for students to read at the start of class. Sometimes I focus my lessons around a quote and use literature to extend the critical thinking aspect of the personal message embedded deep within the quote. Sometimes I just let students ponder the quote without ever making reference to the personal significance. I believe quotes can be used as effective professional development tools, and *Quotes to Inspire Great Reading Teachers* is intended to help teachers accomplish this goal.

—Susan E. Israel, PhD, Assistant Professor,
University of Dayton

Acknowledgments

We are grateful for the many teachers and students who have valued using quotes in the classroom. Since we have always been collectors of quotes and inspirational phrases, we simply can't remember when and where we might have heard some of our favorites. We are grateful for the students from Texas Christian University, The University of Dayton, and the University of Notre Dame who have so graciously inspired us by reviewing our book and inspiring us to select quotes that will inspire great reading teachers. Although we are unable to recall all of you by name or begin to remember which quotes each of you might have shared with us, we still want to thank you for your inspirations. Perhaps we selected certain quotes because they reminded us of some of you.

We want to express deepest appreciation to Ms. JoAnn Zinke, Ms. Cinnamon Whiteley, Ms. Nicole M. Caylor, Ms. Wanda Zinke, Ms. Jenny Hasni, Ms. Rachel Escamilla, Ms. Beth A. Earley, Ms. Molly D. Dahl, Ms. Dixie Massey, Ms. Erin Brianna Doyal, Ms. Sarah M. Luckhaupt, and Ms. Lyndsay Peters for their valuable contributions to this book. We express our joy at having Ms. Jean Ward as the senior acquisitions editor on this project, as without her leadership and vision, this book would have never been published.

Thank you to Cinnamon S. Whiteley for her services related to helping Dr. Block with final edits on the book and with the addition of and modifications to the literature links. Her work has been valuable to the production of the book.

About the Authors

Cathy Collins Block is a professor of education at Texas Christian University. She has taught every grade level from preschool to graduate school, and was elected to serve on the board of directors of the International Reading Association from 2002 to 2005. She has served or is presently serving on the IBM Educational Board of Directors and on the Boards of Directors of the National Reading Conference, the Nobel Learning Communities, and the National Center for Learning Disabilities. She presently serves on the Editorial Boards for the *Journal of Educational Psychology, Reading Research Quarterly, The Reading Teacher, National Reading Conference Yearbook,* and *America Tomorrow.* She has written more than 30 books, including *Reading First and Beyond: The Complete Guide for Teachers and Literacy Coaches* (2005), and 80 research-based articles relative to literacy instruction and teacher education. She has also served or is serving on several elementary and middle school writing teams for public- and private-school textbooks and literacy curriculum materials. She has written for Walt Disney Corporation, PBS television stations, and other national media companies. She has received numerous honors as a teacher, including listings in *Who's Who Among America's Teachers* and *Who's Who in the World.*

Susan E. Israel is graduate reading coordinator and assistant professor at the University of Dayton. In addition, she has served on the Alliance for Catholic Education at the University of Notre Dame. She recently received the Outstanding Professor Award for 2005 from the Panhellenic Council at the University of Dayton. Her publications include another Corwin Press title *Reading First and Beyond: The Complete Guide for Teachers and Literacy Coaches* (2005), as well as a comprehensive volume titled *Metacognition and Literacy Learning* (2005). She is also the author of *Building Collaborative Literacy* (2006) and *Early Reading Pioneers* (2006), and she is working on finishing a book titled *The Rhythm of Poetry* (due to be published in 2006). She researches in developmental aspects of reading comprehension, development of a child's mind, metacognition, how the brain enables reading comprehension, and neuroscience as it relates to reading processes.

*This book is dedicated to my mother and sister, Ms. JoAnn Zinke
and Ms. Wanda Zinke. Their love and support throughout
my life have made it possible for me to give more of my talents
to our profession. For their gifts, I am eternally grateful.*

—*Cathy Collins Block*

*I would like to dedicate this book to my mother, Sandra Berta, and my
mother-in-law, Maureen Israel, for their love and companionship throughout
my life and especially with raising my three daughters, Elizabeth (19), Michelle (17),
and Stephanie (14). Thank you, Mom, for reminding me every day to think
about your favorite quote, "Don't forget to smile."*

—*Susan E. Israel*

Introduction

Susan E. Israel

WHY A BOOK USING QUOTES TO INSPIRE GREAT READING TEACHERS?

As I wrote the proposal that contracted *Quotes to Inspire Great Reading Teachers: A Reflective Tool for Advancing Students' Literacy,* the goal was to create a book with a collection of quotes intended to inspire and assist teachers to reflect on their practices related to literacy development. Inspirational quotes are organized by key components of reading development so that quotes can be included in daily reading lessons to expand students' connections with reading objectives and with their lives outside of school.

- *Making Meaningful Connections* is a collection of quotes that focus on helping teachers reflect on the importance of utilizing background knowledge to make meaningful connections as students learn new concepts.
- *Setting Valuable Goals* is a collection of quotes that develop a deeper understanding both of aspects of literacy acquisition that can be achieved by setting goals and of how the goals can lead to increased achievement and motivation in the classroom.
- *Using Assessment to Excel* is a collection of quotes that make explicit the value of developing assessment experiences throughout life and in literacy experiences by focusing on how assessment is critical to improved reading instruction.
- *Building Blocks for Success* is a collection of quotes organized around the theme of how to increase professional successes and students' literacy successes. The quotes also will aid teachers in reflecting on the many different skills necessary to improve their practices in teaching reading.
- *Word Power Equals Knowledge* is a collection of quotes that emphasize the value of word knowledge and that help teachers reflect on how vocabulary development can be used as a powerful pathway to reading success.

- *Expand Our Opportunity* is a collection of quotes that will help teachers develop an appreciation for how various aspects of reading can expand opportunities in life and literacy learning.
- *Thinking to Obtain Meaning* is a collection of quotes that help teachers reflect on thinking processes that can be improved in order to obtain deeper understanding. These quotes also highlight the fact that meaning making is a critical aspect of literacy development.
- *Identifying Our Strengths* is a collection of quotes that guide teachers in the process of identifying their strengths as teachers. It also encourages the development of students' independence as literacy learners.
- *Work, Study Skills, and Writing* is a collection of quotes that reinforce how writing and study skills can be used as reflective tools. Quotes in this collection can also be used to empower teachers to increase the extent to which students use writing as a tool to increase their literacy accomplishments.
- *Literacy Worlds* is a collection of quotes that help reflect on different cultures and different ways of thinking.
- *Collaborative Communities at School and Home* is a collection of quotes that help teachers place into perspective the benefits of collaboration with people in a variety of learning communities. The quotes in this collection can also aid students in developing a deeper understanding of the value of collaborative communities.

HOW CAN THIS BOOK OF QUOTES BE USED AS A PROFESSIONAL DEVELOPMENT TOOL?

Quotes to Inspire Great Reading Teachers can be a powerful professional development tool in many ways. First, the authors of this book have organized famous, historical, and inspirational quotes in a way that will enable teachers both to deepen reflection and critical thinking and to use the quotes as a tool to think about reading and literacy development.

Second, this book is designed to appeal to a wide range of learning styles and to provide teachers with a creative way to think about their instructional decision making. The impetus for writing the book stems from the need to create a book that uses language as an interactive tool to deepen one's thinking.

Third, this book provides teachers with a guide to document meaningful and personal accounts of their experiences, beliefs, and insight about teaching and literacy development in their classrooms.

Fourth, each lesson includes elements that facilitate reflection, writing, and discussion about literacy. The Lesson Links on each page provide methods of incorporating the quote on that page during reading and other lessons. Many of these Lesson Links are tied to selections of children's literature that reinforce the ideas conveyed in the quote.

WHAT FEATURES ENHANCE REFLECTIVE TEACHING?

Quotes to Inspire Great Reading Teachers includes the following features in each themed collection:

- *Inspirational Quotes.* This is a collection of individual quotes that are organized around central themes to offer teachers fresh ways to develop critical thinking about their professional lives and their students' literacy development.

- *Reading Success Stories.* At the beginning of each collection is a reading success story written by a reading teacher. The stories focus on specific aspects of literacy development; they are true stories of how struggling readers become achieving readers and how struggling teachers grew in their professional practice through reflection and determination to meet the needs of every student.

- *This Quote Makes Me Think About. . . .* This section on each page is a blank space that allows teachers to document and capture their thinking about the quote cited. These comments become a reflective record of professional growth.

- *Prompting Teacher's Deeper Thinking.* Three prompts are provided to help engage the teacher in thinking about the central idea in each quote. The prompts are meant to be used as guides to support teachers thinking about their professional development.

- *Lesson Links.* This boxed section provides questions or lesson ideas teachers can use to inspire students to deepen their thinking and make connections back to the quote.

- *Literature Links.* For most quotes, two related literature selections are provided: one that can be used in Grades K–4 and one for Grades 4–10. The literature selections create additional connections with the theme being described in each chapter. These literature selections are linked with the lessons described in the Lesson Links section. They can be used to increase critical thinking in literacy lessons or in content area instruction.

- *Personal Literacy Goals.* Space to document personal goals is included at the beginning and end of each collection of quotes.

- *My Reading Success.* At the end of each collection of quotes, space is given for teachers to record their own reading success stories of struggling readers or readers who have made accomplishments using the quotes or activities provided in this book.

HOW TO USE THIS BOOK

This book was written to stand alone as a support for teachers in their professional growth as teachers of reading. But it can also serve as a companion book to increase the benefits of using the research-based practices and activities offered in *Reading First and Beyond: The Complete Guide for Teachers and Literacy Coaches* (Block and Israel, 2005).

The individual quotes can be used by teachers with their students to provide a theme for the day and a prompt for metacognitive thinking about their own literacy and learning. It will also expose them to some of our greatest thinkers. Teachers can use the quotes alone, use them with their own journaling instructions to students, or incorporate the additional supports that are provided with each quote for extending students' thinking and connections to literacy content.

In summary, this book can be used to promote and document any teacher's reflection on critical aspects of instruction that help students become great readers. It can be used by individual teachers, teacher teams, or literacy coaches at workshops, inservice trainings, professional development activities, and every day throughout the year.

Themed Collection 1

Making Meaningful Connections

Susan E. Israel,
Sarah M. Luckhaupt,
and Lyndsay L. Peters

READING SUCCESS STORY

The Importance of Making Meaningful Connections

It is difficult for me when I see a child struggling and having a hard time with reading. Future teachers need to think critically about effective methods and develop meaningful practices to work with struggling students. You won't find this in the teaching manuals. The books tell you how and what to teach, but beyond that you need to be creative and think creatively.

Every single child has the capacity for learning. Each child needs to feel important. I believe every child can read at his or her own speed and time. I want every child to feel special or he or she will not perform. My philosophy after 40 years of teaching is very simple. Leave no child behind. Set your expectations high! Children will "stretch" to meet those expectations! I believe and they will achieve.

—Susanne Sullivan, Retired First-Grade Teacher

PERSONAL LITERACY GOALS

Use this space to identify three goals or positive actions you would like to focus on related to inspiring students to make meaningful connections during reading instruction and reading engagements.

66 *What lies behind us and what lies before us are tiny matters compared to what lies within us.* **99**

—Ralph Waldo Emerson

THIS QUOTE MAKES ME THINK ABOUT . . .

PROMPTING TEACHERS' DEEPER THINKING

- What is meaningful to you about being a reading teacher?
- What personal experiences have led you to become a reading teacher?
- What are some issues that you face that keep you from focusing on your inner beliefs about being an effective reading teacher?

LESSON LINKS

1. Ask students about the different ways in which they can think about reading.

2. Who are some of their favorite people who have inspired them to be better readers?

3. Ask students to identify something important that they think keeps them from reading.

LITERATURE LINKS

Grades K–4

Read Anything Good Lately by Susan Allen and Jane Lindaman (2003) is a wonderful book that celebrates the joy of reading by providing ideas of things to read for each letter of the alphabet. Teachers can use this book to help students create their own alphabet books on why reading is important to them.

Grades 4–10

Carver: A Life in Poems by Marilyn Nelson (2001) is a true story about how students can use reading to overcome the emotional and physical challenges that prejudice can cause. This book can be used to introduce Lesson Link #1.

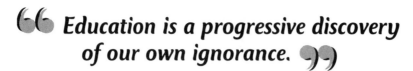

Education is a progressive discovery of our own ignorance.

—Will Durant

THIS QUOTE MAKES ME THINK ABOUT . . .

PROMPTING TEACHERS' DEEPER THINKING

- What does the phrase *progressive discovery* mean to you in relationship to literacy achievement?
- In what areas do you feel you need more knowledge in order to overcome ignorance?
- Reflect on all the memorable books you have read in your life and the progressive path of discovery they have led you to.

LESSON LINKS

1. Ask students what types of books they like to read to advance their interests and overcome their lack of knowledge. Ask them what schools should do to help with overcoming areas of ignorance.

2. Tell students to think about a time they made a progressive discovery; have them describe it in their journals.

3. Have students write about the progressive discoveries made by the main characters in the books they are reading.

LITERATURE LINKS

Grades K–4

You Read to Me, I'll Read to You by Mary Ann Hoberman (2004) is told in two voices; it uses traditional reading techniques and invites students to read along with adults. Older students can use this model to interview classmates and younger students about why reading is important. The book can be used as a model for how to organize two voices.

Grades 4–10

Gershon's Monster by Eric Kimmel (2000) is the story of one boy's journey through a progressive discovery, seeking answers to basic questions about life. Like the book cited above, *Gershon's Monster* can also be used with different voices. It uses different perspectives and special coloring techniques to create a multicultural experience for readers. Have students respond to Lesson Link #3 in pairs after reading this book and discuss it later as a class.

 *Let what you love be what you do.*

—Rumi

THIS QUOTE MAKES ME THINK ABOUT . . .

PROMPTING TEACHERS' DEEPER THINKING

- What do you love about teaching? How can you build more of these types of experiences into your school year?
- What talents would you like to learn about in the future?
- What would your peers say you love to do?

LESSON LINKS

1. Have students list five things they love to do. Ask them what each of these activities has in common.
2. Ask students what types of activities in school they enjoy. Have them explain why they enjoy them so much and what actions they could take to include more of these activities into their school work.
3. After reading, have students list statements in their books that illustrate the characters letting what they loved be what they did.

LITERATURE LINKS

Grades K–4

M Is for Melody: A Music Alphabet, by Kathy-Jo Wargin (2004) is a picture book that focuses on all the different aspects of music. What is nice about this book is that it can be used with several other books written by the author that also focus on what interests students.

Grades 4–10

A Three Minute Speech: Lincoln's Remarks at Gettysburg by Jennifer Armstrong (2003) is a vivid and easy-to-read explanation of the events that led up to the Gettysburg address. It describes that one of the reasons that Lincoln was so successful was that he loved what he did. Complete Lesson Link #3 and ask students to describe why Lincoln loved what he was doing.

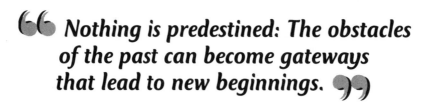

66 *Nothing is predestined: The obstacles of the past can become gateways that lead to new beginnings.* **99**

—Ralph Blum

THIS QUOTE MAKES ME THINK ABOUT . . .

PROMPTING TEACHERS' DEEPER THINKING

- What does *predestined* mean?
- What kind of obstacles have you tried to overcome related to literacy achievement?
- What kind of new things have you tried recently to help students make connections with what you are teaching?

LESSON LINKS

1. Ask students to write about obstacles they have tried to overcome in school.
2. Have students list some of their achievements in reading.
3. Ask students to recall a time when they were beginning a new activity or learning a new skill in reading. What helped them be successful?

LITERATURE LINKS

Grades 4–10

The Three Questions by Jon Muth (2002) is a picture book based on a story by Leo Tolstoy. The three questions asked by the author in the story demonstrate how thinking differently can lead to new beginnings.

> *The mediocre teacher tells. The good teacher explains. The superior teacher demonstrates. The great teacher inspires.*
>
> —William Arthur Ward

THIS QUOTE MAKES ME THINK ABOUT . . .

PROMPTING TEACHERS' DEEPER THINKING

- What does it mean to be a mediocre teacher?
- How do you explain your reading activities?
- In what ways do you think you inspire your students?

LESSON LINKS

1. Ask students what their teachers do that inspires them to read more.
2. Have students write about someone who has helped them be successful in reading.
3. Ask students how they learn best.

LITERATURE LINKS

Grades K–4

Look-Alikes: The More You Look, the More You See by Joan Steiner (2003) is a picture book that uses many unusual illustrations to help students look at things in the world differently. This is a wonderful book that helps build on the notion of discovery and making meaningful connections.

I touch the future. I teach.

—Christa McAuliffe

THIS QUOTE MAKES ME THINK ABOUT . . .

PROMPTING TEACHERS' DEEPER THINKING

- How can you help students touch the future through reading?
- Who is someone who helped you touch the future?
- What is it about teaching you enjoy most?

LESSON LINKS

1. Ask students how they can use reading as a tool to touch the future.

2. Who has helped them touch the future?

3. What do they like the most about learning?

LITERATURE LINKS

Grades K–4

"Oh, the Places You'll Go!" by Dr. Seuss (1990) encourages students to try new things and overcome their fears along the way.

It's not what you are that holds you back . . . but what you think you are not.

—Anonymous

THIS QUOTE MAKES ME THINK ABOUT . . .

PROMPTING TEACHERS' DEEPER THINKING

- What do you do in reading that really motivates students?
- What discouraging reading activities do you think need to be changed or eliminated in order to help students make meaningful connections?
- What holds you back from being the best teacher possible?

LESSON LINKS

1. Ask students what motivates them to work really hard.
2. Have students think of activities they do not enjoy and tell why.
3. Have students identify someone they have read about who has inspired them.

LITERATURE LINKS

Grades K–4

The Diary of a Worm by Doreen Cronin (2003) is a story about all the daily things that a worm does. In this book, students can see how the little things they do help them to become better people and help a lot of things in this world.

Grades 4–10

My Ol' Man by Patricia Polacco (1999) is about discovering people who motivate and inspire. Through the use of storytelling, the author does not merely fill the mind with things that are not important or relevant, but explains the value of learning from those we love.

As teachers we must believe in change, must know it is possible, or we wouldn't be teaching—because education is a constant process of change. Every single time you "teach" something to someone, it is ingested, something is done with it, and a new human being emerges.

—Leo Buscaglia

THIS QUOTE MAKES ME THINK ABOUT . . .

PROMPTING TEACHERS' DEEPER THINKING

- What kind of change do you think is necessary to improve literacy in your school?
- Do you think education is a constant process of change?
- When you teach something, do you ever notice a new human being emerging?

LESSON LINKS

1. Ask students what kinds of changes they have made related to literacy development.
2. Ask them if they like change.
3. Have students consider whether they notice anything different about themselves when their teacher teaches them something.

LITERATURE LINKS

Grades 4–10

Squids Will Be Squids by Jon Scieska and Lane Smith (1998) is a book about fables that develops the concept of change. Through creative words and pictures, students can learn to develop an appreciation for change.

An understanding heart is everything in a teacher, and cannot be esteemed highly enough. One looks back with appreciation to the brilliant teachers, but with gratitude to those who touched our human feeling. The curriculum is so much necessary raw material, but warmth is the vital element for the growing plant and for the soul of the child.

—Carl Jung

THIS QUOTE MAKES ME THINK ABOUT . . .

PROMPTING TEACHERS' DEEPER THINKING

- What does Jung mean when he says that curriculum is a raw material?
- What is an analogy to growing plants in your classroom?
- What reading tasks are meaningful to children in your class?

LESSON LINKS

1. Ask students what raw material is.
2. Have them think about a time they changed someone's life related to literacy.
3. Ask students what teachers can do to help them grow in reading.

LITERATURE LINKS

Grades K–4

Mrs. Spitzer's Garden by Edith Pattou (2001) is about starting the school year by growing plants. Plants in the story go through a wonderful transformation during the year, because the teacher uses lots of tools to cultivate their inner spirits.

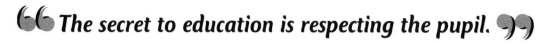

The secret to education is respecting the pupil.

—Ralph Waldo Emerson

THIS QUOTE MAKES ME THINK ABOUT . . .

PROMPTING TEACHERS' DEEPER THINKING

- What positive actions do you portray that demonstrate respect for students?
- What actions do you feel you can add to increase your level of respect?
- What do respecting students and the secret to education have in common?

LESSON LINKS

1. Ask students what positive actions they take to show respect to others who struggle in reading.
2. Have students think about how they can show more respect.
3. Have them identify how they can be respectful when students are learning.

LITERATURE LINKS

Grades K–4

The Day The Babies Crawled Away by Peggy Rathmann (2004) helps students make connections with the concept of showing respect to all children. Watching students is very important, and teachers should observe and converse with students as they engage in new learning experiences. This will enable teachers to ensure that students are making connections between new knowledge—of things that they have never experienced before—and the knowledge they already have of their own world.

The biggest room in the world is the room for improvement. 🙶

—Author Unknown

THIS QUOTE MAKES ME THINK ABOUT . . .

PROMPTING TEACHERS' DEEPER THINKING

- What new teaching techniques have you learned recently?
- What personal experiences have led you to search for new ways of approaching a lesson?
- What are some problems that you run into when attempting to improve a lesson? How can you overcome these problems, or if not overcome them, lessen them?

LESSON LINKS

1. Ask students what subject in school they wish they could improve in and why.
2. Have students name one thing that they can do to improve their understanding of the material in their favorite class.
3. Ask students to consider what motivates them to do their best work.

LITERATURE LINKS

Grades K–4

Hershey's Milk Chocolate Weights and Measures by Jerry Pallotta (2003) is a picture book that uses realistic drawings of Hershey's candy to teach math definitions. This book can help struggling young mathematicians or readers to have fun while they learn. Sometimes a fun way of learning can help a struggling student get motivated to improve. For a struggling reader who loves math, this book is a great resource. The pictures help the student relate to the words on the page.

Teachers can teach, but only students can do something with what they have learned.

—Nick, age 16

THIS QUOTE MAKES ME THINK ABOUT . . .

PROMPTING TEACHERS' DEEPER THINKING

- Do you encourage your students to practice what you have taught them outside of school?
- What activities could you suggest students do outside of the classroom that are homework in disguise?
- How important do you feel it is to connect the material you teach to the real world for your students?

LESSON LINKS

1. Ask students if they have used something outside of school that they enjoyed learning about in school.
2. Have they ever felt that the things they were learning in school would never relate to their lives, but discovered later on that they did?
3. Ask students which subject they would choose and why if there were one subject they had to have homework in every night.

LITERATURE LINKS

Grades 4–10

Chicken Soup For The Preteen Soul by Mark Victor Hansen, Patty Hansen, and Irene Dunlap (2000) capitalizes on young adolescents' interest in reading about real people and their issues. The stories help students become interested in reading because young adolescents live for their social experiences. Students will enjoy reading these stories, while at the same time they will be practicing comprehension skills and other valuable abilities; thus, it becomes homework in disguise.

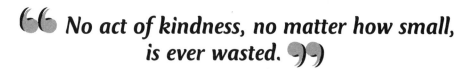

*No act of kindness, no matter how small,
is ever wasted.*

—Aesop

THIS QUOTE MAKES ME THINK ABOUT . . .

PROMPTING TEACHERS' DEEPER THINKING

- How important are acts of kindness in your classroom?
- How can you support acts of kindness among your students?
- How do you show your students that each one is valued equally?

LESSON LINKS

1. Ask students what acts of kindness they have performed in the classroom.
2. How do they feel when someone does something nice for them?
3. How do they feel when someone is unkind to them?

LITERATURE LINKS

Grades 4–10

The Whipping Boy by Sid Fleischman (1986) is a wonderful book for this theme of treating others the way you would want to be treated. In this book Prince Brat, the main character, is taught to be responsible for his own actions and to become empathetic toward others.

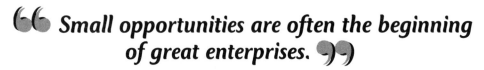

Small opportunities are often the beginning of great enterprises.

—Demosthenes

THIS QUOTE MAKES ME THINK ABOUT . . .

PROMPTING TEACHERS' DEEPER THINKING

- Do you give your students opportunities to help around the classroom?
- Why, or why not, do you feel this is important?
- When you are given opportunities to do something new, how do you feel?

LESSON LINKS

1. Ask students if they have chores at home.
2. Given these jobs to complete, how do students feel?
3. Ask students what other opportunities they are given at school, with friends, etc.

LITERATURE LINKS

Grades 4–10

My Name is Pocahontas by William Accorsi (1992) is a great depiction of what can happen when opportunities present themselves and an individual takes advantage of an opportunity. Students will learn about the Indian princess Pocahontas and how she met John Smith and the other English colonists. Due to her perseverance, she is able to travel to England with them.

Great ability develops and reveals itself increasingly with every new assignment.

—Baltasar Gracian

THIS QUOTE MAKES ME THINK ABOUT . . .

PROMPTING TEACHERS' DEEPER THINKING

- Do you recognize your students' capabilities within their school work?
- How do you acknowledge your students' accomplishments?
- How do you feel about your own accomplishments?

LESSON LINKS

1. Ask students how they feel when they complete an assignment.

2. Which subjects are easy for them and which are more difficult?

3. Have students describe their greatest accomplishments.

LITERATURE LINKS

Grades 4–10

My Side of the Mountain by Jean Craighead George (1959) is a great story which fits in perfectly with this theme. The story is about a boy who lives alone in the mountains, where he learns to adapt to new situations and environments, and is taught an important lesson on survival. Throughout this journey the boy discovers his strengths and weaknesses and learns to use his strengths to survive.

Teachers open the door. You enter by yourself.

—Chinese Proverb

THIS QUOTE MAKES ME THINK ABOUT . . .

PROMPTING TEACHERS' DEEPER THINKING

- What motivated you to become a teacher?
- How do you motivate those students who need more help?
- Who was your most memorable teacher?

LESSON LINKS

1. Ask students what they like most about school, and least.
2. What do they want to be when they are older?
3. Have students describe what motivates them to learn.

LITERATURE LINKS

Grades 4–10

Hiawatha by Henry Wadsworth Longfellow (1983) is a great book to read to get across the theme presented here and to bring some diversity into the classroom. It tells the story of a legendary Native American leader, Hiawatha, and his journey through boyhood to manhood and responsibility. This story allows students to see that, at one time or another, they need to motivate themselves to do things on their own and to become independent.

Learn as much by writing as by reading.

—Lord Acton

THIS QUOTE MAKES ME THINK ABOUT . . .

PROMPTING TEACHERS' DEEPER THINKING

- How important do you feel it is to read the books that your students are reading?
- How much time do you take out for yourself to read and write?
- What are you still learning either from your students or by writing and reading?

LESSON LINKS

1. Ask students if they enjoy writing, and why or why not.
2. Ask students how often they read books outside of school.
3. Do they feel they learn as much by writing as by reading?

LITERATURE LINKS

Grades K–4

Dr. Seuss's ABCs by Dr. Seuss (1963) is a wonderful tool to help beginning readers start to develop some writing skills. This book is designed to help students understand the alphabet through poetic writing.

All kids need is a little help, a little hope, and somebody who believes in them.

—Earvin "Magic" Johnson

THIS QUOTE MAKES ME THINK ABOUT . . .

PROMPTING TEACHERS' DEEPER THINKING

- Do you feel that you instill hope in your students for their future?
- Do you think that your students believe that you have faith in them?
- Do you provide your students with criticism that is hopeless or hopeful?

LESSON LINKS

1. Ask students if they feel the adults in their lives have faith in their success.
2. How hard do they feel they try in school?
3. What subjects do they feel the most frustrated in, and why?

LITERATURE LINKS

Grades 4–10

The Giver by Lois Lowry (1993) is an amazing book that covers hundreds of different themes, and it fits in perfectly with the theme of having someone who believes in you. Jonas is chosen to become the new Receiver of Memories in his town, and the Giver helps him through this painstaking process. The Giver gives Jonas the encouragement he needs to take on this enormous responsibility.

Friends can appear in the most unlikely people, and are often right in front of you. 99)

—Rich Thornton

THIS QUOTE MAKES ME THINK ABOUT . . .

PROMPTING TEACHERS' DEEPER THINKING

- What do you do to encourage your students to befriend each other?
- What is your plan of action when you see a child being left out on a constant basis?
- Is there anything you can do in your classroom to help your students accept each other's differences?

LESSON LINKS

1. Ask students what qualities they look for in a friend.
2. Do they feel that they portray these qualities to their friends?
3. Ask them what they can do to help someone who is left out of a group.

LITERATURE LINKS

Grades 4–10

The Summer of My German Soldier by Bette Greene (1980) deals directly with friendships. It demonstrates to students that two young people, who are supposed to be enemies, can instead put their differences aside and develop compassion, along with trust for one another.

Since you are like no other being ever created since the beginning of Time, you are incomparable.

—Brenda Ueland

THIS QUOTE MAKES ME THINK ABOUT . . .

PROMPTING TEACHERS' DEEPER THINKING

- What makes you unique as a teacher?
- What do you do in your classroom to allow your students to explore their talents?
- What are the special talents of your students, and how do you utilize them in your classroom?

LESSON LINKS

1. Ask students if they have hidden talents.

2. Ask students what they are passionate about.

3. Have students describe their favorite things to do outside of school and why they like these activities so much.

LITERATURE LINKS

Grades 4–10

I'm Gonna Like Me by Jamie Lee Curtis (2002) is a great book that helps students realize their talents. It is dedicated to building self-esteem and loving yourself despite imperfections, because imperfections are what make a person unique.

CLOSING REFLECTIONS

Quotes That Inspire You to Make Meaningful Connections

A Reflection on My Personal Literacy Goals

Use this space to write a reflection on the goals you have achieved or positive actions you have taken related to literacy or reading.

My Reading Success Story

Use this space to document any of your reading success stories.

THEMED COLLECTION 1 BOOK LIST

Accorsi, W. (1992). *My Name is Pocahontas.* New York: Holiday House.

Armstrong, J. (2003). *A Three Minute Speech: Lincoln's Remarks at Gettysburg.* New York: Simon & Schuster.

Cronin, D. (2003). *The Diary of a Worm.* NY: Scholastic, Inc.

Curtis, J. (2002). *I'm Gonna Like Me.* Princeton, NJ: HarperCollins.

Fleischman, S. (1986). *The Whipping Boy.* New York: HarperCollins.

Geisel, T. (Dr. Seuss). (1963). *Dr. Seuss's ABCs.* New York: Random House.

Geisel, T. (Dr. Seuss). (1990). *Oh, the Places You'll Go!* New York: Random House.

George, J. (1959). *My Side of the Mountain.* New York: E. P. Dutton.

Greene, B. (1980). *The Summer of My German Soldier.* New York: Scholastic.

Hansen, M., Hansen, P., & Dunlap, I. (2000). *Chicken Soup For The Preteen Soul.* New York: Scholastic.

Hoberman, M. (2004). *You Read to Me, I'll Read to You.* Boston: Little, Brown.

Kimmel, E. (2000). *Gershon's Monster.* New York: Scholastic.

Lindaman, J., & Allen, S. (2003). *Read Anything Good Lately.* New York: Millbrook Press.

Longfellow, H. (1983). *Hiawatha.* New York: E. P. Dutton. (original edition published 1855)

Lowry, L. (1993). *The Giver.* Boston: Houghton Mifflin.

Muth, J. (2002). *The Three Questions.* New York: Scholastic.

Nelson, M. (2001). *Carver: A Life in Poems.* Asheville, NC: Front Street Press.

Pallotta, J. (2002). *Hershey's Milk Chocolate Weights and Measures.* New York: Scholastic.

Pattou, E. (2001). *Mrs. Spitzer's Garden.* New York: Harcourt.

Polacco, P. (1999). *My Ol'Man.* New York: Putnam.

Rathmann, P. (2004). *The Day The Babies Crawled Away.* New York: Putnam.

Scieska, J., & Smith, L. (1998). *Squids Will Be Squids.* New York: Viking.

Steiner, J. (2003). *Look-Alikes: The More You Look, the More You See.* Boston: Little, Brown.

Wargin, K. (2004). *M Is for Melody: A Music Alphabet.* Chelsea, MI: Sleeping Bear Press.

Themed Collection 2

Setting Valuable Goals

Erin Brianna Doyal and Susan E. Israel

READING SUCCESS STORY

The Importance of Setting Goals

"A student is born with wings, but a teacher shows how to use them to fly." I thought this was an excellent quote by Shelby Stollery because all students are able to learn no matter if they are on an IEP, mentally challenged, or simply disengaged. As it has been pounded in our heads, we must remember to have high expectations for all students.

I have already seen this happen in my field work. I had a student in one of my classes who had a terrible home life and received no academic support outside of school. My cooperating teacher was having difficulty with this student and I was as well when I began my teaching unit. I noticed that he never really paid attention to the lessons I was teaching so I decided to get him more involved. When I did experiments or activities, I always made sure he was involved in some way and he took to this. He began showing interest, raising his hand, and even sharing his thoughts on why these experiments happened regardless if he was wrong or right.

It was still difficult to get him to read, but I found his strength and latched on to it. We must do this for every student and never give up until we have reached them all. I have one tip for anyone who teaches science and is looking for great informational picture books. Look no further than any book done by Seymour Simon. He also has science mystery books if you are a language arts teacher and looking to integrate a little science.

—Daniel Szeremet, Fifth-Grade Science,
Literacy, and Social Studies Teacher

PERSONAL LITERACY GOALS

Use this space to identify three goals or positive actions you would like to focus on related to inspiring students to set valuable goals during reading instruction and reading engagements.

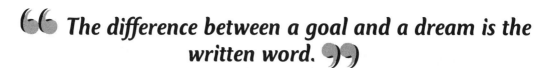

The difference between a goal and a dream is the written word.

— Gene Donohue

THIS QUOTE MAKES ME THINK ABOUT . . .

PROMPTING TEACHERS' DEEPER THINKING

- How does the written word elevate the abstract to the concrete?
- What "unwritten" dreams can you turn into goals?
- Why do students often hide their goals from the people around them?

LESSON LINKS

1. Ask students how the act of goal setting can become the basis for personal writing.

2. After reading the quote and *Winners Never Quit,* have students write a journal entry about how they handle frustrations. Have them create a list of different ways they would advise a friend on handling frustrations.

3. What do students think is the difference between a goal and a dream? They will have new answers to question after reading *Go for the Goal: A Champion's Guide to Winning Soccer and Life.*

LITERATURE LINKS

Grades K–4

Winners Never Quit by Mia Hamm (2004) is a particularly nice approach to helping kids understand how to handle frustration. After reading, ask students to respond to Lesson Link #2 above.

Grades 4–10

Go For the Goal: A Champion's Guide to Winning Soccer and Life by Mia Hamm (2000) is an inspiring book for boys and girls alike that intermixes goal setting and soccer into a lively read. Sections might be read aloud to slightly lower grades with success. This book can be paired with Lesson Link #3; have students discuss responses as a class.

You got to be careful if you don't know where you're going, because you might not get there. 99

—Yogi Berra

THIS QUOTE MAKES ME THINK ABOUT . . .

PROMPTING TEACHERS' DEEPER THINKING

- Who determines where you are going as a teacher?
- What aspects of your teaching do you feel need direction?
- How can you help your students determine direction for their own lives?

LESSON LINKS

1. Have students write a paragraph imagining where they want to be next week, then another about next year.

2. Ask students to think about a time they missed an opportunity because they weren't prepared to take it. They can use the book in the Literature Link K–4 below to help.

3. Have students create a goal journal so they can track their dreams and successes. They can use the book in the Literature Link below (for Grades 4–10) to help.

LITERATURE LINKS

Grades K–4

Ramona Quimby, Age 8 by Beverly Cleary (1992) is about a lovable and realistic character who illustrates how kids can overcome frustrations and obstacles to achieve their goals. Ask students to respond to Lesson Link #2 in pairs and to reveal a time when they have missed an opportunity.

Grades 4–10

Making Every Day Count: Daily Readings for Young People on Solving Problems, Setting Goals, and Feeling Good About Yourself by Pamela Espeland and Elizabeth Verdick (1998) contains a realistic and motivational approach to goal setting that provides specific helpful ideas for older students. This book can be used as a nonfiction selection. After sharing the main idea with students, have them begin working on Lesson Link #3.

It takes great goals to lead us out of our everyday limits into accomplishing more than we ever thought we could or would.

—Robert Cooper

THIS QUOTE MAKES ME THINK ABOUT . . .

PROMPTING TEACHERS' DEEPER THINKING

- What great goals have you already accomplished?
- What are the everyday limits that prevent you from reaching your goals?
- What limits can you remove from your students' school experience?

LESSON LINKS

1. What things or people currently limit your future opportunities?
2. Do you have control over any of the obstacles preventing you from reaching your dreams?
3. Draw a picture of your greatest accomplishment in life so far.

LITERATURE LINKS

Grades K–4

The Tale of Despereaux by Kate Dicamillo (2003) is an adorable modern fairy tale about the adventures of a big-eared mouse. It makes a wonderful read-aloud that will spur lively conversations about dreams and risk taking. Have each student complete Lesson Link #3 individually.

Grades 4–10

First & Goal by Dan Marino (1997) is an excellent book with vivid pictures and an inspiring lesson about not giving up no matter the odds. Teachers may use this book to reach young boys who are reluctant to read and to complete Lesson Link #2.

*If you want to live a happy life,
tie it to a goal—not to people or things.*

—Albert Einstein

THIS QUOTE MAKES ME THINK ABOUT . . .

PROMPTING TEACHERS' DEEPER THINKING

- How do you define happiness?
- Do you substitute things for the active pursuit of happiness?
- How can you help your students understand the happiness that is gained from hard work, not possessions?

LESSON LINKS

1. Have students write about the lessons they have learned from getting caught or getting into trouble.

2. Ask students to recall a time when they accomplished a goal they were particularly proud of achieving. Have them write a story about this time—*Peaches,* below, can give them some story ideas.

3. Have students draw a comic strip starring people who have lots of material things but are still unhappy.

LITERATURE LINKS

Grades K–4

Peaches by Jodi Lynn Anderson (2005) is an adventurous story for a young audience. Ask students to write a story about a time they were once in trouble and what lessons they learned from their mistakes.

Grades 4–10

A Taste-Berry Teen's Guide to Setting and Achieving Goals by Bettie and Jennifer Youngs (2002) is a sweet book composed of short stories about kids. While the book as a whole is intended for older students, many of the stories can be used with younger students. Have students respond to Lesson Link #2 after reading a story from this book.

The tragedy of life doesn't lie in not reaching your goal. The tragedy lies in having no goal to reach.

—Benjamin Mays

THIS QUOTE MAKES ME THINK ABOUT . . .

PROMPTING TEACHERS' DEEPER THINKING

- How does goal setting help shape the course of your life?
- Would your life look different if you used goals to determine its path?
- Does the fear of failure ever prevent you from striving for your dreams?

LESSON LINKS

1. Ask students why they think setting goals is significant in having a successful life.
2. Have students write about the person whose accomplishments they admire most and explain why.
3. Have students create a collage of the things that are important to them.

LITERATURE LINKS

Grades K–4

David's Secret Soccer Goals by Caroline Levine (2004) is a sweet book that deals with sensitive issues, such as bed-wetting, and explores how to overcome obstacles. Students can respond to *David's Secret Soccer Goals* by completing Lesson Link #3.

Grades 4–10

We Beat the Street: How a Friendship Pact Led to Success by Sharon Draper (2005) is a wonderful book about overcoming obstacles, written by an award-winning author. This is an excellent nonfiction book that teaches valuable lessons while telling an action filled story. Have students complete Lesson Link #2 individually.

*Acceptance of prevailing standards
often means we have no standards of our own.* 🙶🙶

—Jean Toomer

THIS QUOTE MAKES ME THINK ABOUT . . .

PROMPTING TEACHERS' DEEPER THINKING

- Who sets the standards in your classroom?
- Are you satisfied with meeting the state standards?
- How can you involve students in setting standards for themselves?

LESSON LINKS

1. Ask students, "Who sets the standards?" for the quality of their work.
2. Have students write a list of simple standards for writing in their classroom.
3. Ask students how often they evaluate their personal standards.

LITERATURE LINKS

Grades K–4

I Can Ride It by Shigeo Watanabe (1982) is a picture book that relates realistic childhood frustrations with a positive ending and uplifting illustrations. Have students create a picture of an image in their mind when the teacher reads this story.

Grades 4–10

A Single Shard by L. S. Park (2001) is a useful reading to go along with this quote. Have students complete Lesson Link #2 as a class, and post the standards in the classroom after reading this book.

66 *The reason most people never reach their goals is that they don't define them, or ever seriously consider them as believable or achievable. Winners can tell you where they are going, what they plan to do along the way, and who will be sharing the adventure with them.* **99**

—Denis Watley

THIS QUOTE MAKES ME THINK ABOUT . . .

PROMPTING TEACHERS' DEEPER THINKING

- How well defined are your classroom goals?
- Do you have specific expectations for your professional development?
- Can you take a currently vague goal and make it more specific?

LESSON LINKS

1. Have students decide as a class what makes someone a winner.

2. Ask students to share their adventures and goals with those around them.

3. Ask students if they take their own goals seriously. Have them explain.

LITERATURE LINKS

Grades K–4

The Blue Ribbon Day by Katie Couric (2004) is an energetic book that takes a look at childhood frustrations. Its vivid illustrations will captivate young readers while the text will inspire them to explore their own talents. As a class, have students respond to the question in Lesson Link #1 after reading this book.

Grades 4–10

Isabelle Lives a Dream by Peggy Sundberg (2003) features the cowgirl character Isabelle, who will be loved by young girls who are interested in horses. Have students respond to Lesson Link #3 in journals.

Our goals can only be reached through the vehicle of a plan, in which we must fervently believe, and upon which we must vigorously act. There is no other route to success.

—Stephen A. Brennan

THIS QUOTE MAKES ME THINK ABOUT . . .

PROMPTING TEACHERS' DEEPER THINKING

- What goals do you have that do not yet have a specific plan of action?
- How can students be encouraged to develop ways to achieve their goals?
- Do you believe you can achieve your dreams?

LESSON LINKS

1. Ask students to write a haiku on the theme "Success."

2. Have students create a plan of action for one of their current literacy goals.

3. Have students ask themselves, "Where is my route to success?"

LITERATURE LINKS

Grades K–4

Inches and Miles: The Journey to Success by John R. Wooden (2003) is about an inchworm and a mouse who set out on an adventure; kids who read it will learn about working toward a dream. After reading this book as a class, ask each student to work on Lesson Link #2, and post the goals in the classroom.

Grades 4–10

Reaching Your Goals by Robin Silverman (2004) has lots of quotes from students on how to set and reach realistic goals. It provides a good starting point for any kid wanting to improve him or herself. For a different activity to pair with this book, have students complete Lesson Link #1.

Without goals, and plans to reach them, you are like a ship that has set sail with no destination. 🙶🙶

—Fitzhugh Dodson

THIS QUOTE MAKES ME THINK ABOUT . . .

PROMPTING TEACHERS' DEEPER THINKING

- In what other ways can taking a journey be a metaphor for your goals?
- Does your teaching have direction?
- How can you create a map of your future by setting specific goals?

LESSON LINKS

1. Have students write a metaphor for the goals they have set for themselves.

2. Ask students to draw a map of their goals. Have them set a course from their current place to their anticipated destination.

3. As students what their goals are for their education.

LITERATURE LINKS

Grades K–4

Tony's Hard Work Day by Alan Arkin (2002) is a delightful picture book in which little Tony surprises his family by bypassing their low expectations of his abilities. It is an excellent choice for helping students see that they can determine their own potential. After reading this book, have students create a map of their goals as described in Lesson Link #2.

Grades 4–10

Hairy Britches: Goal Setting Techniques by Ragnar the Viking by Beley Raidt (1996) is a funny book with great illustrations and interesting facts about Vikings. It provides a unique approach to teaching lessons about goals that can be used with any age group. After reading this book, students can work on their own to complete Lesson Link #1.

I try to avoid looking forward or backward, and try to keep looking upward.

—Charlotte Bronte

THIS QUOTE MAKES ME THINK ABOUT . . .

PROMPTING TEACHERS' DEEPER THINKING

- As teachers, do we spend more time looking forward or backward?
- How can you look upward in life?
- What can we do to help our students let go of past disappointments?

LESSON LINKS

1. Ask students what things from the past they find themselves dwelling on.
2. Ask students what you can do to help them reach their personal goals.
3. Have students write a poem about expectations.

LITERATURE LINKS

Grades K–4

The Mole With a Goal by Tracy Kompelien (2004) is a fun rhyming book that raises the issue of goals through the playful antics of its title character. Meet with each of your students individually to discuss Lesson Link #2.

Grades 4–10

Pursue Your Goals by Eric Lindros (1999) includes personal reflections on the sport of hockey, among which students will find motivational messages to inspire them to pursue their own goals. In small groups or independently, have students complete Lesson Link #3, and make a poster to show their poems to the class.

CLOSING REFLECTIONS

Quotes That Inspire You to Set Valuable Goals

A Reflection on My Personal Literacy Goals

Use this space to write a reflection on the goals you have achieved or positive actions you have taken related to literacy or reading.

My Reading Success Story

Use this space to document any of your reading success stories.

THEMED COLLECTION 2 BOOK LIST

Anderson, J. (2005). *Peaches.* New York: HarperCollins.

Arkin, A. (2002). *Tony's Hard Work Day.* Layton, UT: Gibbs Smith.

Cleary, B. (1992). *Ramona Quimby, Age 8.* New York: HarperCollins.

Couric, K. (2004). *The Blue Ribbon Day.* New York: Doubleday.

Dicamillo, K. (2003). *The Tale of Despereaux.* Cambridge, MA: Candlewick Press.

Draper, S. (2005). *We Beat the Street: How a Friendship Pact Led to Success.* London: Puffin.

Espeland, P., & Verdick, E. (1998). *Making Every Day Count: Daily Readings for Young People on Solving Problems, Setting Goals, and Feeling Good About Yourself.* Minneapolis, MN: Free Spirit.

Hamm, M. (2000). *Go For the Goal: A Champion's Guide to Winning Soccer and Life.* New York: HarperCollins.

Hamm, M. (2004). *Winners Never Quit.* New York: HarperCollins.

Kompelien, T. (2004). *The Mole With a Goal.* Edina, MN: Abdo.

Levine, C. (2004). *David's Secret Soccer Goals.* Philadelphia, PA: Jessica Kingsley.

Lindros, E. (1999). *Pursue Your Goals.* Lanham, MD: Taylor.

Marino, D. (1997). *First & Goal.* Lanham, MD: Taylor.

Park, L. (2001). *A Single Shard.* New York: Clarion Books.

Raidt, B. (1996). *Hairy Britches: Goal Setting Techniques by Ragnar the Viking.* Nashville, TN: Winston-Derek.

Silverman, R. (2004). *Reaching Your Goals.* London: Franklin Watts.

Sundberg, P. (2003). *Isabelle Lives a Dream.* Irvine, CA: Coyote Moon.

Watanabe, S. (1982). *I Can Ride It.* London: Philomel Books.

Wooden, J. (2003). *Inches and Miles: The Journey to Success.* Des Moines, IA: Perfection Learning.

Youngs, B., & Youngs, J. (2002). *A Taste-Berry Teen's Guide to Setting and Achieving Goals.* Deerfield Beach, FL: HCI Teens.

Themed Collection 3

Using Assessment to Excel

Dixie Massey

READING SUCCESS STORY

The Importance of Using Assessment to Excel

Maintaining a teaching journal proved to me the value of reflection. In the past I have started journals but have always been sidetracked by the many demands of a classroom teacher. In rereading my journal, I realize that it provides a social history of my teaching this year. As I read it again and again, I have new reflections and insights into my teaching practice, my values, and my beliefs. It points the way to new areas of concern. My teaching journal is not only a document that records the places that I have been—it also points directions to the places that I have yet to go.

—Mrs. Webb, Third-Grade Teacher

PERSONAL LITERACY GOALS

Use this space to identify three goals or positive actions you would like to focus on related to using assessment to excel in your own practices and using assessment to help your students excel.

Obstacles are those frightful things you see when you take your eyes off the goal.

—Henry Ford

THIS QUOTE MAKES ME THINK ABOUT . . .

PROMPTING TEACHERS' DEEPER THINKING

- How do you successfully assess whether you have kept your eyes on the goal?
- Identify several obstacles that keep you from being able to focus on developing students' love of literature and reading.
- What obstacles made you a better teacher?

LESSON LINKS

1. Have students describe a time that they or someone else overcame an obstacle. Ask them what helped them overcome that obstacle.

2. Have them set a personal reading goal for the week.

3. Have students create their own speech about something they believe in and how they know their belief helps them reach their goals.

LITERATURE LINKS

Grades K–4

First Flight: The Story of the Wright Brothers by Caryn Jenner (2003) is the story of the Wright brothers. This biography tells how the brothers experienced many obstacles as they tried to create the first airplane. Teachers can use this book to help students learn the importance of focusing on goals as described in Lesson Link #2.

Grades 4–10

Brother Eagle, Sister Sky: A Message From Chief Seattle by Chief Seattle and Susan Jeffers (1991) has beautiful paintings that are the backdrop for Chief Seattle's speech to those who wanted to buy his native Northwest land. This speech offers several opportunities to talk about truths we have learned and how we have learned these truths. After reading this book, have students individually complete Lesson Link #3.

My only advice is to stay aware, listen carefully, and yell for help when you need it. 🙶

—Judy Blume

THIS QUOTE MAKES ME THINK ABOUT . . .

PROMPTING TEACHERS' DEEPER THINKING

- What advice would you give novice teachers about assessing their own teaching of reading?
- Think of some different people who might help the struggling readers in your class.
- Keep a journal of what your students say to you. Review it frequently to assess how you stay aware of your students' needs.

LESSON LINKS

1. Ask students about the best advice someone ever gave them.
2. How do they know when to yell for help?
3. What advice do they have for beginning readers?

LITERATURE LINKS

Grades K–4

Olivia by Ian Falconer (2000) is about a main character, Olivia, who learns several things, including about art and how to build a sand castle. Students could be encouraged to imitate the drawings and use of color in the books to illustrate their own stories. Have students create a list of books for beginning readers.

Grades 4–10

Leonardo da Vinci by Diane Stanley (1996) is a description of da Vinci's work and of all the things that he was interested in, and even of some of his failures. This is a great book for reading to students to spark their own interests and confirm the importance of trying again. In pairs, have students discuss Lesson Link #2 and come up with a plan on how they can offer help to someone who does not ask for it.

Success is never final; failure is never fatal. It is courage that counts.

—Winston Churchill

THIS QUOTE MAKES ME THINK ABOUT . . .

PROMPTING TEACHERS' DEEPER THINKING

- How are failure and success measured in reading achievement? In what other ways can you measure failure and success in your classroom?
- What is the purpose of courage? How do we demonstrate courage in our teaching?
- Describe a student who has shown courage.

LESSON LINKS

1. Ask students what courage reminds them of. Ask them to explain why it is important.
2. What goals would they like the courage to pursue?
3. Ask students how becoming a good reader requires courage.

LITERATURE LINKS

Grades K–4

Jungle Drums by Graeme Base (2004) describes a young warthog who uses courage to tell the truth. This book fits nicely with a theme on courage, allowing students to explore when other people have needed courage. After reading *Jungle Drums,* have the class work on personal goals and share their goals with a classmate so they can be held accountable for that goal.

Grades 4–10

The Rag Coat by Lauren Mills (1991) describes how several families in Appalachia came together to help a little girl without a father. It exemplifies how we can help and learn from each other. It is a wonderful book to explore the universal theme of courage and acceptance and can be used to work on Lesson Link #1.

66 *The ultimate test of teaching is not what you do or how well you do it, but what and how well the learner does.* 99

—Howard Hendricks

THIS QUOTE MAKES ME THINK ABOUT . . .

PROMPTING TEACHERS' DEEPER THINKING

- Reflect on how you learned to read and who influenced your reading development.
- How does your teaching today reflect the teachers in your past?
- What do you hope your students will do that reflects your teaching?

LESSON LINKS

1. Ask students how learning and teaching are alike.

2. Have them describe themselves as learners.

3. Have students identify some things that teachers do to help them learn.

LITERATURE LINKS

Grades K–4

The Mountain That Loved a Bird by Alice McLerran (2000) is a book which illustrates the power of small things to bring great changes. After reading this book, students can work on Lesson Link #2; then ask them to create a contract describing how they will change the way they do things in order to always give their best.

Grades 4–10

The Velveteen Rabbit by Margery Williams (1958) offers a beautiful description of inner changes as we become real. Teachers can use this book to help students reflect on the importance of sharing ourselves with others and to discuss Lesson Link #1 as a class.

What is our praise or pride but to imagine excellence and try to make it.

—Richard Wilbur

THIS QUOTE MAKES ME THINK ABOUT . . .

PROMPTING TEACHERS' DEEPER THINKING

- How can we help readers imagine excellence?
- What do you think is the importance of teacher modeling to help students excel?
- How do you encourage students to demonstrate excellence in your classroom?

LESSON LINKS

1. Ask students to describe a time they have set a goal and worked hard to attain it. How did they evaluate their success?

2. How do they imagine excellence as a reader?

3. Ask students what event in history or in their life they learned the most from.

LITERATURE LINKS

Grades K–4

Snowflake Bentley by Jacqueline Briggs Martin (1998) tells the story of the man who first photographed snowflakes, discovering that each snowflake is different. Mr. Bentley was relentless in his curiosity and quest to understand science and to share his discoveries with the world. His biography provides an excellent illustration of setting goals and striving for them. After reading this story, ask students to work on Lesson Link #1.

Grades 4–10

Of Mice and Men by John Steinbeck (1994) is a classic tragedy. This is an excellent book to read before responding to Lesson Link #3 in a class discussion or small-group discussion.

Kind words can be short and easy to speak but their echoes are truly endless.

—Mother Teresa

THIS QUOTE MAKES ME THINK ABOUT . . .

PROMPTING TEACHERS' DEEPER THINKING

- What have you read that still echoes with you?
- What words would you hope echo with your students?
- How are kind words important when assessing student reading?

LESSON LINKS

1. Ask students what kind words they remember a teacher saying to them. Why do they remember these words?
2. What do they think Mother Teresa meant when she said that the "echoes are truly endless"?
3. Have students pick out a few of their favorite quotes or lines from the story they read. Ask them why they selected those and what the lines or quotes mean to them.

LITERATURE LINKS

Grades K–4

Chrysanthemum by Kevin Henkes (1996) is a perfect example of the influence of kind words. Chrysanthemum is discouraged when other students in her class make fun of her name, but when a teacher compliments Chrysanthemum's name, Chrysanthemum is encouraged and the other students' criticism is silenced. Students might create a "kind words" book in the classroom to encourage positive comments to each other. Respond to Lesson Link #2.

Grades 4–10

The Catcher in the Rye by J. D. Salinger (1991) is an entertaining read for all ages. This classic story is one for students who are entering adolescence. After completing this story, ask students to work on Lesson Link #3 and discuss their findings with a partner.

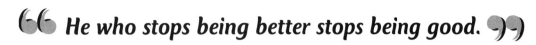

He who stops being better stops being good.

—Oliver Cromwell

THIS QUOTE MAKES ME THINK ABOUT . . .

PROMPTING TEACHERS' DEEPER THINKING

- What have you purposely done to improve your personal knowledge of both academic and other areas?
- How does your personal knowledge influence your ability to assess students?
- What could you do that would make you a better reader?

LESSON LINKS

1. Ask students what they have learned recently. Have them explain how what they learned made them better at something.
2. Ask them what things have made them better readers since they first learned to read.
3. Ask students how assessment can help them gain knowledge.

LITERATURE LINKS

Grades K–4

Lotsa de Casha by Madonna (2005) is a colorful read about a wealthy man who reminds us all of a very valuable lesson—money does not buy happiness. In small groups or pairs, students can respond to this book by answering questions for Lesson Link #1.

Grades 4–10

Pride and Prejudice by Jane Austen (1995) reflects on the effects of old-fashioned social customs on the English aristocracy. This reflection will assist students to understand how social customs affect their lives as well. Students will also be able to identify with one of the many characters in this classic tale. In response to the story have students answer Lesson Link #1 in journals.

Education should equip a person to live life well, to understand what is happening about him, for to live life well one must live with awareness. 99

—Louis L'Amour

THIS QUOTE MAKES ME THINK ABOUT . . .

PROMPTING TEACHERS' DEEPER THINKING

- What do you think "equip" refers to when teaching reading?
- What is the role of awareness in teaching and assessing students?
- What goals and measures do you have for understanding what is happening in your classroom?

LESSON LINKS

1. Ask students to identify a teacher who modeled how to live life well.
2. Ask students what awareness they have gained from the selection the class is reading.
3. After reading, have students describe three valuable insights they have about living with greater awareness.

LITERATURE LINKS

Grades K–4

In My Family by Carmen Garza (2000) provides opportunities for students to value the small events of another culture. It also serves as a model for students to use to share their own family stories. After reading *In My Family*, have students begin working on Lesson Link #3.

Grades 4–10

The Story of George Washington Carver by Eva Moore (1990) describes the many things that George Washington Carver was interested in and how these interests helped him overcome oppression to help others. Have students discuss Lesson Link #2 as a class. Ask them to record a few of the responses on a sheet of paper and explain why they agree or disagree with their classmates.

CLOSING REFLECTIONS

Quotes That Inspire You to Use Assessment to Excel

A Reflection on My Personal Literacy Goals

Use this space to write a reflection on the goals you have achieved or positive actions you have taken related to literacy or reading.

My Reading Success Story

Use this space to document any of your reading success stories.

THEMED COLLECTION 3 BOOK LIST

Austen, J. (1995). *Pride and Prejudice.* London: Penguin. (original work published 1813)

Base, G. (2004). *Jungle Drums.* New York: Harry N. Abrams.

Falconer, I. (2000). *Olivia.* New York: Simon & Schuster.

Garza, C. (2000). *In My Family.* San Francisco: Children's Book Press.

Henkes, K. (1996). *Chrysanthemum.* New York: HarperTrophy.

Jeffers, S., & Seattle, Chief (1991). *Brother Eagle, Sister Sky: A Message From Chief Seattle.* New York: Dial Books.

Jenner, C. (2003). *First Flight: The Story of the Wright Brothers.* New York: DK Publications.

Madonna. (2005). *Lotsa de Casha.* London: Callaway.

Martin, J. (1998). *Snowflake Bentley.* Boston: Houghton Mifflin.

McLerran, A. (2000). *The Mountain That Loved a Bird.* New York: Simon & Schuster.

Mills, L. (1991). *The Rag Coat.* New York: Little, Brown.

Moore, E. (1990). *The Story of George Washington Carver.* New York: Scholastic.

Salinger, J. (1991). *The Catcher in the Rye.* New York: Little, Brown. (original work published 1945)

Stanley, D. (1996). *Leonardo da Vinci.* New York: HarperCollins.

Steinbeck, J. (1994). *Of Mice and Men.* London: Penguin. (original work published 1937)

Williams, M. (1958). *The Velveteen Rabbit.* New York: Doubleday.

Themed Collection 4

Building Blocks for Success

Cathy Collins Block and Cinnamon S. Whiteley

READING SUCCESS STORY

The Importance of Building Blocks for Success

I enjoy helping children learn to see themselves as word explorers. To come across an unknown word is an opportunity for an adventure. It is so much fun to show my students the many places they can look for treasure such as dictionaries, context, root words, and other word parts. I've found that when my students see a word search as an opportunity rather than as an obligation, they become more engaged and persistent when they encounter new words. Even now, at the age of 39, I can't wait to run to a dictionary to discover the meaning of a word that is new to me. I try to show that excitement to my students. For me, once a child becomes a word explorer, then he will be truly unleashed to explore wherever his dreams take him.

—Mrs. Parris, Middle School Teacher

PERSONAL LITERACY GOALS

Use this space to identify three goals or positive actions you would like to focus on related to using building blocks to foster student success during reading instruction and reading engagements.

❝ I have missed more than 9,000 shots in my career. I have lost almost 300 games. On 26 occasions I have been entrusted to take the game-winning shot and I missed. I have failed over and over again in my life. And that's precisely why I succeed. ❞

—Michael Jordan

THIS QUOTE MAKES ME THINK ABOUT . . .

PROMPTING TEACHERS' DEEPER THINKING

- Think of a student who you are trying to help become a better reader. What have you tried? What can you try that you have just created?
- Describe one teacher who inspires you to keep teaching.
- What areas cause frequent failures in reading for your students?

LESSON LINKS

1. Ask students what makes people good at what they do.
2. Ask students what they could do to become better readers.
3. Have students describe something that they do that they have to practice doing.

LITERATURE LINKS

Grades K–4

Wolf by Becky Bloom (1999) describes how a wolf visits a farm where animals read. The wolf doesn't know how to read, so he must first learn to read. Then he discovers that he is not very good at reading until he practices. Students can interview a family member to discover something that the family member had to practice doing.

Grades 4–10

Tomas and the Library Lady by Pat Mora (2000) tells the true story of Tomas Rivera, who was a child of migrant workers and became a university president. The story is about the influence that a librarian had on Dr. Rivera's life. Creating a timeline of an influential person's life can help students recognize the obstacles that many people have overcome.

Let us not be content to wait and see what will happen, but give us the determination to make the right things happen.

—Peter Marshall

THIS QUOTE MAKES ME THINK ABOUT . . .

PROMPTING TEACHERS' DEEPER THINKING

- Is there a situation in which you have been content to wait to see what happens but in which you might have wanted to make the right things happen instead?
- What kind of obstacles have you tried to overcome related to your own or your students' literacy achievement?
- What kind of new things have you tried recently to help students make "the right things happen" in reading?

LESSON LINKS

1. Have students write about obstacles they try to overcome in school. Ask them what new ideas they get from reading one of these books listed below.
2. Ask them about their achievements in reading.
3. Have students recall a time when they were beginning a new activity or learning a new skill in reading. Ask what helped them be successful at this.

LITERATURE LINKS

Grades K–4

The Empty Pot by Demi (1990) describes how truth is always the best tool against obstacles. It also shows how people can face adversity with truth and courage which leads them to a new beginning. In your journals respond to Lesson Link #1.

Grades 4–10

Zen Shorts by Jon Muth (2005) is a picture book that is a Caldecott Honor book and contains several short stories in which the main characters do the right thing. It can be used to open a discussion of all three Lesson Links above.

I did no more than others did, I don't know where the change began, I started as an average kid, I finished as a thinking man.

—Rudyard Kipling

THIS QUOTE MAKES ME THINK ABOUT . . .

PROMPTING TEACHERS' DEEPER THINKING

- How do you ensure your students will have a successful year at the beginning of the academic year?
- How do you prepare for a successful school year?
- How do you develop average kids to be thinkers?

LESSON LINKS

1. Ask students what becoming a thinker means to them and how they might feel the change.

2. Have students write about a time when they felt success as a thinker.

3. Ask students in what ways they celebrate and learn from their successes.

LITERATURE LINKS

Grades K–4

The English Roses by Madonna (2003) is a story of friendship and how we must all learn who we are and how we want others to see us. Have students individually complete Lesson Link #2 after reading this book.

Grades 4–10

The Story of Sony by Aaron Frisch (2003) is about the beginnings of one of the most famous and well-known electronic companies in the world—Sony. After reading this book, ask students to write their goals and the steps involved to ensure they will be successful in meeting them. Lesson Link #3 would also be an excellent assignment to pair with this book. Students can partner with a classmate and discuss with their peers how they would celebrate after succeeding.

Perseverance is a great element of success. If you only knock long enough and loud enough at the gate, you are sure to wake up somebody.

—Henry Wadsworth Longfellow

THIS QUOTE MAKES ME THINK ABOUT . . .

PROMPTING TEACHERS' DEEPER THINKING

- Do you model perseverance for your students?
- What other characteristics contribute to success?
- How do you teach perseverance to your students who struggle?

LESSON LINKS

1. Ask students what it takes to persevere.

2. Have students list two things that it takes to be successful.

3. Have students name a gate to their success as a reader and describe how they can "knock loud and hard" to obtain success.

LITERATURE LINKS

Grades K–4

The Little Engine That Could by Watty Piper, George Hauman, and Doris Hauman (1976) is a timeless story of determination and perseverance. As a class have students answer Lesson Link #3 and record students' responses.

Grades 4–10

Ella Enchanted by Gail Carson Levine (1998) tells the story of a strong female who reaches goals by overcoming obstacles through determination. Ask students to answer Lesson Link #3 on their own and then form groups to discuss the steps involved in reaching a goal.

When you make an error, don't dwell on it and don't excuse it; value the correction.

—Connie Eddieman

THIS QUOTE MAKES ME THINK ABOUT . . .

PROMPTING TEACHERS' DEEPER THINKING

- Do you teach your students to learn from their mistakes?
- What are you doing to help your students overcome their struggles in reading?
- Are you understanding when your students are honest about not understanding certain steps or when they ask you to repeat the instructions?

LESSON LINKS

1. Have students identify the feelings they dealt with when they last made a mistake or an error.

2. Ask students if they value their failures as much as their successes. Have them explain.

3. Ask them to explain whether they persevere after they have failed.

LITERATURE LINKS

Grades K–4

Mistakes That Worked by Charlotte Foltz Jones and John O'Brien (1994) is a book that provides a sample of the many successes and products that ironically are created by mistake. This story is a great lead to a new activity and can be used with Lesson Link #1.

Grades 4–10

Song of the Trees by Mildred D. Taylor (2003) is a story that deals with real issues that today's Generation Y students face. This author's purpose is to send the message that it is important to support each other so that more dreams can be achieved. Have students discuss Lesson Link #1 in groups and then select a speaker for the group to summarize the feelings the group discussed. Students may also volunteer to discuss a situation when others supported them in achieving their dreams, or the teacher may reveal such a situation.

What is a weed? A plant whose virtues have not yet been discovered.

—Ralph Waldo Emerson

THIS QUOTE MAKES ME THINK ABOUT . . .

PROMPTING TEACHERS' DEEPER THINKING

- Do you discuss with your students their successes? How often?
- How do you encourage your students who realize their peers have understood a lesson and they have not?
- Do you bring literature into the classroom that explores and deals with diversity? How often and why?

LESSON LINKS

1. Ask students what they have discovered about themselves. How did they do this?

2. Do they think we are all "weeds" at the beginning of our lives? Ask them to explain in what ways we are weeds.

3. Discuss with students what they do to uncover what is special and unique about themselves.

LITERATURE LINKS

Grades K–4

Ordinary Splendors: Tales of Virtues and Wisdoms by Toni Knapp (1994) is a book of tales compiled from around the world. Each tale teaches students how people in a specific culture discover things about themselves through events or rites of passages. Educators can have students write or draw pictures about characters of their choice who they think have a special quality that is revealed in an adventure.

Grades 4–10

The Land by Mildred D. Taylor (2001) contains a story that stresses the importance of our values and being true to them. After reading this book students can write about Lesson Link #2 as an entry in their journals.

> **" *To achieve a purpose or goal a person must have the courage to attempt it, and the faith that he can accomplish it. What the mind can conceive and perceive the mind can achieve.* "**

—William Arthur Ward

THIS QUOTE MAKES ME THINK ABOUT . . .

PROMPTING TEACHERS' DEEPER THINKING

- What goals did you set at the beginning of the school year?
- Do you teach your students to visualize their goals?
- In what ways do you give students courage to attempt difficult tasks?

LESSON LINKS

1. Discuss with students the meaning of courage.

2. Ask them what steps they take to encourage themselves to reach for their goals.

3. Ask students to think about how much courage it takes to reach for their dreams. Have them explain why this takes courage.

LITERATURE LINKS

Grades K–4

Call It Courage by Armstrong Sperry (1971) is a story about a young boy who finds courage in himself to conquer a fear. This story is a great way to begin a discussion on what it takes to follow your dreams. Educators can use this book as a tool to prompt students to list their dreams, their goals, and what might keep them from reaching their goals.

Grades 4–10

A Corner of the Universe by Ann Martin (2002) reminds students of challenges they may have faced already and gives them a glimpse of challenges they will be facing in the future. As adults we know that we are better people because of the challenges we have faced. Educators can pair this book with Lesson Link #2 and have students write a personal essay on it.

Knowledge advances by steps and not by leaps.

—Lord Thomas Babington Macaulay

THIS QUOTE MAKES ME THINK ABOUT . . .

PROMPTING TEACHERS' DEEPER THINKING

- Have you recently tried to learn something new, and do you remember the frustration you dealt with?
- Do you share these types of experiences with your students? How?
- In what ways do you think you encourage your students when they are struggling and become frustrated by learning a new skill or unit?

LESSON LINKS

1. Ask students if they try to learn new things for every school year.
2. How do they continue learning over the summer?
3. How do they stay motivated to continue learning new things?

LITERATURE LINKS

Grades K–4

The Secret Knowledge of Grown-Ups by David Wisniewski (2001) tells about many of the actions that adults take and the reasons that they do so. Reading this book is a great way to encourage students at the end of the school year. It helps students more clearly understand the reasoning behind the actions of adults. It also gives reason behind the way they talk to children. After reading this book together as a class, students can discuss Lesson Link #2 as a class.

Grades 4–10

Hoot by Carl Hiaasen (2004) contains unusual characters but students will still be able to relate to them. Students can respond to Lesson Link #3 by sharing in small groups and reporting their responses to the class.

Doing the best in this moment puts you in the best place for the next moment.

—Oprah Winfrey

THIS QUOTE MAKES ME THINK ABOUT . . .

PROMPTING TEACHERS' DEEPER THINKING

- How do you inspire your students to do their best?
- When was the last time you remember working hard toward an important goal? What could you do to teach your life lessons to your students?
- Do you teach your students about the steps that lead to success? Do you remind them that success does not happen overnight?

LESSON LINKS

1. Ask students how they model doing their best. Have students create a play or write about it.
2. Ask students what it means to do their best.
3. How do they prepare for success and learn from their failures?

LITERATURE LINKS

Grades K–4

The Princess Knight by Cornelia Funke and Kerstin Meyer (2004) is a story about a young girl who perseveres and believes in herself to show the world that she can be a knight even though she is a girl. This book is an inspiration to those who feel they could not try out for a sport or join a club. It teaches readers that if they put their mind to something they can accomplish it.

Grades 4–10

Cinderella Man: James Braddock, Max Baer, and the Greatest Upset in Boxing History by Jeremy Schaap (2005) is a book that many students, especially boys, have expressed pleasure in reading. Read this book to help children visualize how to model doing their best, then have students write a play about a time they did their best.

Give the world the best you have, and the best will come back to you.

—Madeline Bridges

THIS QUOTE MAKES ME THINK ABOUT . . .

PROMPTING TEACHERS' DEEPER THINKING

- Do you give your students your best every day? What strategy could you recommend to new teachers that could help them overcome difficult days?
- How do you tell your students that their work is not their best?
- Do you encourage your students daily, weekly, or only when you see a moment to let them know they should do their best? Why? Be prepared to share your answers in a grade-level meeting or faculty meeting.

LESSON LINKS

1. Ask students if they give their best at the beginning and at the end of the school year. Have them describe a time when they gave their best and something good they did not expect came back to them.
2. Have students describe why good things happen to good people.
3. Do they believe that if they give their best that it pays off in the end? Why or why not?

LITERATURE LINKS

Grades K–4

The Talent Show From the Black Lagoon by Mike Thaler and Jared D. Lee (2004) is a story about how literary characters band together to create the best performance possible. This story is for educators who need a book to help students understand how they can become their best even when they do not have material support to help them.

Grades 4–10

Crispin: The Cross of Lead by Avi (2002) is a story that contains many obstacles and challenges. This book can help students learn why it is important to give their best at all times; it can be read in conjunction with Lesson Link #3 above.

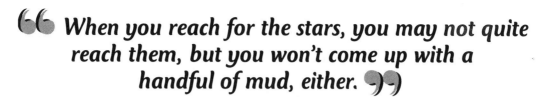

When you reach for the stars, you may not quite reach them, but you won't come up with a handful of mud, either.

—Leo Burnett

THIS QUOTE MAKES ME THINK ABOUT . . .

PROMPTING TEACHERS' DEEPER THINKING

- Do you think it is important to teach children how to accept failure and recognize partial success?
- How do you handle failure?
- Do you think failing at something can teach as valuable a lesson as succeeding? Write about a recent professional success and a professional failure. On a new sheet of paper, create two columns of what you learned from each: Which did you grow from the most, and what does this tell you about how you learn?

LESSON LINKS

1. Ask students how they felt when they worked really hard but did not win first place. Have them list in two columns: "What Is Gained From Working Hard and Not Winning" and "What Is Lost From Working Hard and Not Winning."

2. Have students describe what they felt like when they came in second or third that was different from when they came in first. Help them to identify the benefits of coming in less than first, and the drawbacks of coming in first for winners who are not prepared for success.

3. Ask students to discuss people they have known who benefited from reaching for the stars. Have them identify and list the traits that these people have in common.

LITERATURE LINKS

Grades K–4

There Was a Bold Lady Who Wanted a Star by Charise Mericle Harper (2002) is an adventurous story. This story inspires students to think about what they really want and what they are willing to do to attain it. It can be read before you discuss Lesson Link #3 above.

Grades 4–10

The View From Saturday by E. L. Konigsburg (1998) contains such a strong moral that students will learn lessons for life. It describes what is possible when you do not accept failure, and it can be used with Lesson Link #2 above.

Each dawn holds a new hope for a new plan, making the start of each day the start of new life.

—Gina Blair

THIS QUOTE MAKES ME THINK ABOUT . . .

PROMPTING TEACHERS' DEEPER THINKING

- Do you think that each day is full of new possibilities? Why?
- What does it mean to seize the day?
- Do you seize each day with your students, family, and friends?

LESSON LINKS

1. Ask students what they can do to increase their abilities to seize the day every day.
2. Have students write about what they do to make each school year better than the year before.
3. How do they feel when someone gives them a second chance? Do they think people should offer second chances? Have them describe the answers to both of these questions.

LITERATURE LINKS

Grades K–4

Tough Beginnings: How Baby Animals Survive by Marilyn Singer and Anna Vojtech (2001) describes the beginnings of baby animals' lives. It shows that even babies must overcome obstacles as early as minutes after birth in order to survive and to experience life. Students can each pick an animal to learn about and find out what difficulties the young of that animal may experience. Read this book to introduce Lesson Link #2 above.

Grades 4–10

Missing May by Cynthia Rylant (1992) discusses feelings and emotions all of us have when we experience grief and loss. It is important for students to learn how to deal with emotions and feelings, and this book is a great lead for a discussion about Lesson Link #3 above.

CLOSING REFLECTIONS

Quotes That Inspire You to Build Blocks for Success

A Reflection on My Personal Literacy Goals

Use this space to write a reflection on the goals you have achieved or positive actions you have taken related to literacy or reading.

My Reading Success Story

Use this space to document any of your reading success stories.

THEMED COLLECTION 4 BOOK LIST

Avi. (2002). *Crispin: The Cross of Lead.* New York: Hyperion.

Bloom, B. (1999). *Wolf.* New York: Scholastic.

Demi. (1990). *The Empty Pot.* New York: Henry Holt.

Frisch, A. (2003). *The Story of Sony.* N. Mankato, MN: Smart Apple Media.

Funke, C. & Meyer, K. (2004). *The Princess Knight.* Somerset, UK: The Chicken House.

Harper, C. (2002). *There Was a Bold Lady Who Wanted a Star.* New York: Megan Tingley.

Hiaasen, C. (2004). *Hoot.* New York: Knopf.

Jones, C., & O'Brien, J. (1994). *Mistakes That Worked.* New York: Doubleday.

Knapp, T. (1994). *Ordinary Splendors: Tales of Virtues and Wisdoms.* Lanham, MD: Roberts Rinehart.

Konigsburg, E. (1998). *The View From Saturday.* New York: Simon & Schuster.

Levin, G. (1998). *Ella Enchanted.* New York: HarperTrophy.

Madonna. (2003). *The English Roses.* London: Callaway.

Martin, A. (2002). *A Corner of the Universe.* New York: Scholastic.

Mora, P. (2000). *Tomas and the Library Lady.* New York: Random House.

Muth, J. (2005). *Zen Shorts.* New York: Scholastic.

Piper, W., Hauman, G., & Hauman, D. (1976). *The Little Engine That Could.* New York: Platt & Munk. (original edition published 1930)

Rylant, C. (1992). *Missing May.* New York: Orchard Books.

Schaap, J. (2005). *Cinderella Man: James Braddock, Max Baer, and the Greatest Upset in Boxing History.* Boston: Houghton Mifflin.

Singer, M., & Vojtech, A. (2001). *Tough Beginnings: How Baby Animals Survive.* New York: Henry Holt.

Sperry, A. (1971). *Call It Courage.* Hampshire, UK: MacMillan.

Taylor, M. (2001). *The Land.* London: Dial.

Taylor, M. (2003). *Song of the Trees.* London: Puffin Books.

Thaler, M., & Lee, J. (2004). *The Talent Show From the Black Lagoon.* Madison, WI: Turtleback Books.

Wisniewski, D. (2001). *The Secret Knowledge of Grown-Ups.* New York: HarperTrophy.

Themed Collection 5

Word Power Equals Knowledge

Cathy Collins Block,
Cinnamon S. Whiteley,
and Nicole M. Caylor

READING SUCCESS STORY

The Importance of Word Power

I once read how Dr. Martin Luther King Jr. defined success. He said, "We are prone to judge success by the index of our salaries or the size of our automobiles, rather than by the quality of our service and our relationship to humanity." As I look back over the 36 years of my teaching career, I see the smiling, laughing, contemplating, glowing faces of child after child whose lives touched my soul, and through whom I have received riches beyond compare.

I have also heard many times that to attain the highest levels of success one must make one's vocation one's avocation. While I agree that the most successful teachers I have known approach their profession with boundless passion, energy, and dedication, I have found that there is another quality common to the truly greatest teachers in the world. Mark Twain best described this essential element when he said, "The secret of success is making your vocation your vacation." As I recall all the exemplary teachers that changed my life as a student and with whom I've worked as an adult, they all infused boundless enthusiasm, joy, pleasure, and fun into the professional actions they took. When they walked into a group, spirits were lifted and the arduousness of a task vanished.

We wrote this chapter about word power with one thought in mind. We wanted you to have time to reflect on several qualities that have proven to advance teachers to higher levels of achievement. It is our goal that by the time you have completed this chapter, through your deep reflection, you will have (a) improved the quality of your service, (b) deepened your relationship to humanity, and (c) increased your ability to awaken every day in excited anticipation of the joys that your teaching can bring to you and your students.

—Cathy Collins Block, Professor
at Texas Christian University

PERSONAL LITERACY GOALS

Use this space to identify three goals or positive actions you would like to focus on related to word power and word knowledge and to how students can learn about this during reading instruction and reading engagements.

We must open the door of opportunity. But we must also equip our people to walk through those doors.

—Lyndon B. Johnson

THIS QUOTE MAKES ME THINK ABOUT . . .

PROMPTING TEACHERS' DEEPER THINKING

- How long do you spend on a unit, a skill, or a concept?
- Do you equip students by reviewing concepts and repeating new words often?
- How do you think your students learn best? Why?
- How does word knowledge equip students to walk through doors?

LESSON LINKS

1. Ask students how they prepare themselves to learn new information. They should think about whether they remember more if they learn it by listening, talking, reading, writing, or doing. Have them select their best method of learning and describe in journals a time when they learned a lot because of it.
2. Discuss with students why word power equals knowledge.
3. Ask students to describe their interests in writing or orally.

LITERATURE LINKS

Grades K–4

Inkheart by Cornelia Funke (2003) is an exciting book through which students can exercise their creativity in a world filled with vivid images and drama. Educators can use this book as an example of how words can capture readers and send them to another world. It can be read as students complete Lesson Link #2 above.

Grades 4–10

The Thief Lord by Cornelia Funke and Oliver Latsch (2002) has been read by numerous students in our classrooms. They have rated it as one of the best mysteries that they have ever read. As they read this book, have students consider which learning method is the main character's best one and why. This book can be used in conjunction with Lesson Link #1 above.

Words are of course, the most powerful drug used by mankind.

—Rudyard Kipling

THIS QUOTE MAKES ME THINK ABOUT . . .

PROMPTING TEACHERS' DEEPER THINKING

- What words or quotes guide your life? Who taught this philosophy to you?
- What quotes inspire you? Why?
- Write your philosophy of teaching in one word below. What did this activity illustrate to you about the power of one word? Share the word you wrote and the thoughts you have about the power of words with students.

LESSON LINKS

1. Ask students what powerful messages or words they say to get their way and what their words illustrate about the truth in today's quote.
2. Ask students to think about whether their vocabulary is as powerful as it could be and why it is important to gain power from words.
3. Have students describe a person they know who uses the power of words. Ask them if that person's use of words makes the person more powerful. Have them explain.

LITERATURE LINKS

Grades K–4

The Giving Tree by Shel Silverstein (1964) enables students to learn about the power of communication. Students can discuss how the use of more powerful communication could have created a better ending for both the boy and the tree (as well as others). Discuss the power of words in this book after students have written or discussed Lesson Link #1 above.

Grades 4–10

The Wizard of Oz Vocabulary Builder by Mark Phillips (2003) contains 1,850 challenging vocabulary words that can be used to help students prepare for standardized tests and for life. Have students discuss Lesson Link #3 in groups.

I like a teacher who gives you something to think about besides homework.

—Lily Tomlin

THIS QUOTE MAKES ME THINK ABOUT . . .

PROMPTING TEACHERS' DEEPER THINKING

- What words do you share with your students to motivate them? Are there more powerful and varied words you can use?
- What did you give your students to think about today that they will think about 10 years from today?
- How can you build more time in your daily schedule to discuss life-changing ideas?

LESSON LINKS

1. Have students write a list of quotes that inspire them; keep the list at hand for the days or mornings they need a little pick-me-up.
2. Have students write a personal story about a moral they have learned.
3. Ask students what books they enjoy reading in their free time.

LITERATURE LINKS

Grades K–4

The Children's Book of Virtues by William J. Bennett (1995), former secretary of education, introduces basic mores of American culture through stories, poems, and fables. This book illustrates the power of words differently than the other books mentioned by tying them to specific moral lessons. This book can be used to introduce Lesson Link #2 above.

Grades 4–10

The Pinocchio Intermediate Vocabulary Builder by Mark Phillips (2004) contains 1,000 vocabulary words that are likely to occur often in textbooks for Grades 4–10. The vocabulary words appear in bold type in every story, and their definitions appear at the bottom of each page. They are easy to understand. Ask students to combine two or more of these words to create a sentence that conveys an important powerful idea about their lives.

Every passage has its price.

—Meredith Ann Pierce

THIS QUOTE MAKES ME THINK ABOUT . . .

PROMPTING TEACHERS' DEEPER THINKING

- In this dark quote, the word *passage* has two meanings. What are they and how can you teach both meanings of this quote to students?
- Which passage in your life costs you the most?
- Which passage in a book contained such powerful words that your life changed as a result?

LESSON LINKS

1. Have students copy a passage from a book that they have read and explain why it is their favorite.
2. Ask students how words and knowledge can help them overcome difficulty in the passages of their lives. Have students discuss this in groups.
3. Ask students if they think we admire heroes because they pay a price for success. Have them explain.

LITERATURE LINKS

Grades K–4

The Cat in the Hat by Dr. Seuss (1957) shows how many English words have similar spellings. It enables students to develop word recognition and to use more specific words in their conversations. Ask students to select their favorite pages from this (or another book) and tell why they were favorites. See Lesson Link #1 above.

Grades 4–10

Tarzan and Jane's Guide to Grammar by Mark Phillips (2005) is a book that students enjoy because Jane is charged with the task of teaching Tarzan how to speak more effectively. She teaches him about grammar so that he can write. Use this book as an example of how words are "heroes" to reach success, as described in Lesson Link #2 above.

A poet can survive anything but a misprint.

—Oscar Wilde

THIS QUOTE MAKES ME THINK ABOUT . . .

PROMPTING TEACHERS' DEEPER THINKING

- Do you remember a time when someone misunderstood what you had to say and misinterpreted it? What will you do in the future when you are misunderstood and why?
- What is the one thing you as a teacher could not survive and why?
- Use this quote to open a poetry unit. Discuss why it is true.

LESSON LINKS

1. Play telephone. Tell one student a phrase or a quote quietly so no one else can hear; then ask that student to tell the next student what he or she heard quietly. Allow for each student to pass on the phrase or the quote and have the last student say out loud what was heard. Is what was said by the last student the same phrase or quote you originally said?

2. Read *Carver: A Life in Poems* by Marilyn Nelson (2001) (see Chapter 1). This book illustrates how incidents in famous people's lives can be conveyed powerfully through poetry. Ask students to select a hero of theirs. Have students read about that person or interview that person and then relate a significant event in that person's life through poetry.

3. Ask students to write a poem about something that they have accomplished that was important in their lives.

LITERATURE LINKS

Grades K–4

Little Bill's Big Book of Words by Catherine Lukas, Bill Cosby, and Robert Powers (2002) is one of a series of books about Little Bill. Bill Cosby's goal in writing them was to help children value aspects of their lives and to gain skills that will serve them throughout their lives. This one aids students in developing a full understanding of the meaning behind words. It can be used as an example of the power of words, and in conjunction with Lesson Link #1 above.

Grades 4–10

Powerful Words: More Than 200 Years of Extraordinary Writings by African Americans by Wade Hudson (2004) describes African American culture throughout the years in which discrimination occurred against them. Students can use this book to help them better understand how to vividly express themselves using the power of words. This book is an excellent book to use in Lesson Link #2 above.

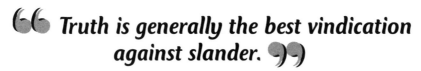

Truth is generally the best vindication against slander.

—Abraham Lincoln

Justice is truth in action.

—Benjamin Disraeli

Truth is the secret of eloquence and virtue, the basis of moral authority; it is the highest summit of art and of life.

—Henri Frederic Amiel

THESE QUOTES MAKE ME THINK ABOUT . . .

PROMPTING TEACHERS' DEEPER THINKING

- Do you always tell the truth?
- What have you learned in the above quotes concerning the power of words to increase your truthfulness?
- When would you not tell the truth? Why?

LESSON LINKS

1. Ask students how they justify not telling the truth.

2. After students read the quotes as a class, discuss the actions people can take to use the power of truth-filled words more frequently.

3. Have students think of a literary character that told the truth and write what they learned from that figure.

LITERATURE LINKS

Grades K–4

The Many Adventures of Johnny Mutton by James Proimos (2001) describes how language assisted the main character whenever he entered new situations. Students will have fun learning how language can assist them too. This book could be read before assigning Lesson Link #3. Did any of the characters in this book have to tell the truth?

Grades 4–10

The Friendship by Mildred Taylor (1998) is a story that will help students better appreciate their friends. This book is excellent to use at the beginning or end of working on Lesson Link #3 above.

Sharp words make more wounds than a surgeon can heal.

—Thomas Churchyard

THIS QUOTE MAKES ME THINK ABOUT . . .

PROMPTING TEACHERS' DEEPER THINKING

- Do you often say things in the heat of anger?
- What can you do and teach students to do to overcome the detrimental effects of powerful words spoken in anger?
- Do you forgive people when they apologize for saying the wrong thing?

LESSON LINKS

1. Ask students if they forgive their friends or families when things are said in anger but not meant.
2. Have students describe the best things people can do to ask for and receive forgiveness.
3. Ask students how they feel when they are reading a book and the main character uses words to help others. Ask them what this means about the power of words and the effects they have on how people feel about you.

LITERATURE LINKS

Grades K–4

Larky Mavis by Brock Cole (2001) is a book in which students can see the power of choosing the correct words. It is an excellent book to read to the class for Lesson Link #3 above.

Grades 4–10

Martin's Big Words: The Life of Dr. Martin Luther King Jr. by Doreen Rappaport (2001) describes one of Martin Luther King Jr.'s most important skills. He had the ability to choose just the right word. It explains that as a child he listened to his father's "big words," and it demonstrates again the effect that words have on an individual. You can ask students to select their favorite words that Dr. King used and later have students respond to Lesson Link #3.

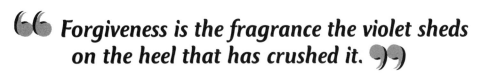

Forgiveness is the fragrance the violet sheds on the heel that has crushed it.

—Mark Twain (Samuel Clemens)

THIS QUOTE MAKES ME THINK ABOUT . . .

PROMPTING TEACHERS' DEEPER THINKING

- Do you treat each day as a fresh start for you and your students? What steps can you take to ensure you do?
- Write the deeper meaning of this quote.
- Are there students you need to forgive you? Explain.

LESSON LINKS

1. Discuss with your students what it means to forgive a friend, a family member, or an adult in their lives.
2. Have students write a riddle using the sentence structure of today's quote that defines a powerful word that is important to them. Share riddles in class by posting them in the room for everyone to read and use to learn new words.
3. Have students reread a poem or prose that they wrote earlier in the year. Have them work in pairs to select more vivid, powerful words for each other's writings. Select a few to share as "before" and "after" examples with the class.

LITERATURE LINKS

Grades K–4

Riddle Roundup: A Wild Bunch to Beef Up Your Word Power by Giulio Maestro (1989) includes 62 riddles to introduce young readers to new words and encourage them to use words they already know in different ways. This is a great activity book for the primary grades. The riddles would best be used in a classroom activity. This book is an excellent book to introduce Lesson Link #2 above.

Grades 4–10

Fooling With Words: A Celebration of Poets and Their Craft by Bill Moyers (1999) is a collection of interviews of American poets that will help students learn how poets use words powerfully to communicate. This is a great tool for the upper school classroom because it demonstrates to students how much work goes into writing with powerful words. This book is excellent for use with Lesson Link #3.

This above all: to thine own self be true, and it must follow, as the night the day, thou canst not then be false to any man.

—William Shakespeare

THIS QUOTE MAKES ME THINK ABOUT . . .

PROMPTING TEACHERS' DEEPER THINKING

- What can you do to remove any artificial barriers you may have inadvertently created between yourself and your students? What parts of your personality and abilities to relate to your students do you most value? Can you use these to build a clear image of all that you are for your students?
- Is there a definite situation or time in the school day when you feel as if you are performing a role rather than being yourself? Why? What can you do to convey more of the truth about yourself in these situations during these times? What benefits will your new, more truth-filled actions bring to you and your students?
- What action can you take to change this situation or yourself? Meet with students this week whom you feel are having difficulty being true to themselves or being themselves in a certain settings. Listen to their ideas about why and advise.

LESSON LINKS

1. Ask students what it means to be true to themselves. Have them describe the circumstances or things that surround the times when they feel as if they are being people they are not. Ask them what they could do to overcome this difficulty.
2. Have students describe why it is better to be true to themselves than to feel as if they have to be people they are not.
3. Have students select another quotation (from Shakespeare or from those you have discussed in class) and rewrite it in their own words. Ask them to explain why the words they choose were more powerful to them than the words chosen by the original authors.

LITERATURE LINKS

Grades K–4

Vocabulary Repair Kit: Improve Your Word Power by Angela Burt, William VanDyck, and David Farris (2002) was written to assist students in improving their vocabularies. This book provides students with a lens through which to see the worth behind possessing such word power, and it can be used as a part of Lesson Link #3.

Grades 4–10

Shakespeare's Flowers by Francie Owens (2001) shows students how the bard looked at nature and events from a perspective that was different from that of others. His use of words enables students to see anew the strength of "word power." This is a great book for students to read independently or to read aloud as part of Lesson Link #3.

With the passage of years we must take care that our dreams do not become regrets.

—JoAnn Zinke

THIS QUOTE MAKES ME THINK ABOUT . . .

PROMPTING TEACHERS' DEEPER THINKING

- Do you have any regrets about teaching?
- What is the biggest professional dream that you have? What step could you take to help it come true?
- How do you carve out time (away) from your daily teaching duties to ensure that you create the opportunity for your dreams to become reality and not regrets?

LESSON LINKS

1. Ask students what dreams they have. Discuss ways they can make their dreams come true.

2. Ask students about dreams they have had in the past that came true. Ask them what actions they took to help their dreams come true.

3. Read about a main character whose dream came true. On one side of a sheet of paper have students list all the actions that person took to make the dream come true. On the other side of the paper, have them list all the actions they themselves have taken to make their own dreams come true. Ask students to compare these lists and discuss what they learned.

LITERATURE LINKS

Grades K–4

Lisa's Airplane Trip by Anne Gutman and George Hallensleben (2001) is a humorous book. It demonstrates how words can affect our emotions and lead us to become happy. This book can be paired with Lesson Link #3.

Grades 4–10

On My Honor by Marion Dane Bauer (1987) is a story that we recommend that you read aloud. It shows how powerful and meaningful words can be and is a great book to introduce Lesson Link #3.

CLOSING REFLECTIONS

Quotes That Inspire You to Use Word Power to Gain Knowledge

A Reflection on My Personal Literacy Goals

Use this space to write a reflection on the goals you have achieved or positive actions you taken related to literacy or reading.

My Reading Success Story

Use this space to document any of your reading success stories.

THEMED COLLECTION 5 BOOK LIST

Bauer, M. (1987). *On My Honor.* Boston: Houghton Mifflin.

Bennett, W. (1995). *The Children's Book of Virtues.* NY, Simon & Schuster.

Burt, A., VanDyck, W., & Farris, D. (2002). *Vocabulary Repair Kit: Improve Your Word Power.* London: Hodder & Stoughton.

Cole, B. (2001). *Larky Mavis.* New York: Farrar, Straus and Giroux.

Funke, C. (2003). *Inkheart.* Somerset, UK: The Chicken House.

Funke, C., & Latsch, O. (2002). *The Thief Lord.* Somerset, UK: The Chicken House.

Geisel, T. (Dr. Seuss). (1957). *The Cat in the Hat.* New York: Random House.

Gutman, A., & Hallensleben, G. (2001). *Lisa's Airplane Trip.* New York: Knopf Books.

Hudson, W. (2004). *Powerful Words: More Than 200 Years of Extraordinary Writings by African Americans.* New York: Scholastic.

Lukas, C., Cosby, B., & Powers, R. (2002). *Little Bill's Big Book of Words.* New York: Simon & Schuster.

Maestro, G. (1989). *Riddle Roundup: A Wild Bunch to Beef Up Your Word Power.* Boston: Clarion Books.

Moyers, B. (1999). *Fooling With Words: A Celebration of Poets and Their Craft.* New York: William Morrow–HarperCollins.

Owens, F. (2001). *Shakespeare's Flowers.* New York: Michael Friedman.

Phillips, M. (2003). Wizard of Oz Vocabulary Builder. Bayside, NY: A. J. Cornell.

Phillips, M. (2004). *The Pinocchio Intermediate Vocabulary Builder.* Bayside, NY: A. J. Cornell.

Phillips, M. (2005). *Tarzan and Jane's Guide to Grammar.* Bayside, NY: A. J. Cornell.

Proimos, J. (2001). *The Many Adventures of Johnny Mutton.* San Diego, CA: Harcourt Children's Books.

Rappaport, D. (2001). *Martin's Big Words: The Life of Dr. Martin Luther King, Jr.* New York: Hyperion.

Silverstein, S. (1964). *The Giving Tree.* New York: HarperCollins.

Taylor, M. (1998). *The Friendship.* London: Puffin.

Themed Collection 6

Expanding Our Opportunity

Cathy Collins Block and Cinnamon S. Whiteley

READING SUCCESS STORY

The Importance of Expanding Opportunity

As a young teacher, I hold strong beliefs to not give up on any child. I strive to give children opportunities that others would think the child would never be able to achieve. I find many teachers are stuck with a strategy and do not try to utilize new strategies. I have observed teachers who try to hold onto their favorite strategy even when they see that it is not effective with every child. Many teachers stick to a one-size-fits-all policy. Instead, teachers should take the time to evaluate each child's particular needs and try to find a strategy that will suit their individual learning style.

—Mrs. Williams, Special Education Teacher

PERSONAL LITERACY GOALS

Use this space to identify three goals or positive actions you would like to focus on related to inspiring students to expand their opportunities and to how they can learn about this during reading instruction and reading engagements.

Action that is clearly right needs no justification.

—Elisabeth Elliot

THIS QUOTE MAKES ME THINK ABOUT . . .

PROMPTING TEACHERS' DEEPER THINKING

- What actions do you justify?
- What does justification mean?
- Are you always right and others wrong?

LESSON LINKS

1. Ask students if they give their friends a chance to justify their actions.
2. What does *justify* mean to them?
3. Ask students if they think they are ever wrong.

LITERATURE LINKS

Grades K–4

What to Do When You're Scared and Worried: A Guide for Kids by James J. Crist (2004) enables you to ask students about what fears they have in the classroom and about their abilities. Have students write in their journals about their fears in the classroom.

Grades 4–10

Get Off My Brain: A Survival Guide for Lazy Students by Randall McCutcheon (1997) is a guide to suggestions you can use to motivate students and teach them the value of being efficient. Have students discuss Lesson Link #2 in pairs.

If you want to lift yourself up, lift up someone else.

—Booker T. Washington

THIS QUOTE MAKES ME THINK ABOUT . . .

PROMPTING TEACHERS' DEEPER THINKING

- Do you find new opportunities to do better, to be better, and to teach better? What is common to these situations? What do these commonalities tell you about what you need to be your best?
- How do you use this truth to become a strong classroom leader? State a way in which everyone at your school can lift colleagues up often and routinely.
- Do you encourage others in your life outside of school?

LESSON LINKS

1. Ask students what opportunity they have in which they most want to do better. Have them explain how they could use the truth in today's quote to help them do this.

2. Tell students that some of the strongest leaders in our country use the truth in this quote to reach big goals. Have students read about a leader they admire and write how the leader lives the truth of today's quotation.

3. As a class, select a project and develop a plan by which everyone can work together to help someone or some cause outside of school. When the project is finished have students discuss how they feel and explain why.

LITERATURE LINKS

Grades K–4

Tough Cookie by David Wisniewski (1999) is an inspirational book that demonstrates that we can achieve anything. This book can be used with Lesson Link #2 above.

Grades 4–10

Combinations: Opening the Door to Student Leadership by Ed Gerety (2003) reveals to teenagers what one must do to become a leader. After they read this book, ask students to work on Lesson Link #2 as a writing assignment for class work or homework.

Life affords no greater responsibility, no greater privilege, than the raising of the next generation. **99**

—C. Everett Koop

THIS QUOTE MAKES ME THINK ABOUT . . .

PROMPTING TEACHERS' DEEPER THINKING

- What does responsibility and privilege mean to you? Why?
- What is your greatest responsibility?
- Do you feel that you help raise your students?

LESSON LINKS

1. Ask students what responsibilities they have when they are in your class.
2. Discuss the responsibilities they have at home.
3. Ask students if they think it is necessary to have responsibilities.

LITERATURE LINKS

Grades K–4

Teaching to Change Lives: Seven Proven Ways to Make Your Teaching Come Alive by Howard Hendricks (2003) is a guide to help teachers make the most of their classroom time to touch the lives of all of their students. Have your students complete a KWL *(What I Know, What I Want to Know, and What I Learned)* chart with this book.

Grades 4–10

Poetry by Heart compiled by Liz Attenborough (2001) has many poems which demonstrate how students can expand their own worlds by acting on opportunities as they present themselves. Have students complete Lesson Link #3 in their journals.

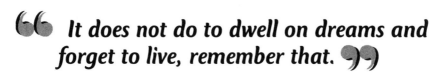

It does not do to dwell on dreams and forget to live, remember that.

—J. K. Rowling

THIS QUOTE MAKES ME THINK ABOUT . . .

PROMPTING TEACHERS' DEEPER THINKING

- Do you dwell on problems? Why?
- Do you live your life to its fullest? How?
- What does it mean to forget to live?

LESSON LINKS

1. Ask students if they have dreams that keep them from living.
2. Ask what they neglect to do while dreaming.
3. Ask them how they can evaluate whether they are balancing living and dreaming.

LITERATURE LINKS

Grades K–4

Carnival at Candlelight by Mary Pope Osborne and Sal Murdocca (2005) is filled with beautiful photographs. Its stories have heroes and plots that vividly display the power of capitalizing on every opportunity. It can also be used to show students how to write their own stories. Have students respond to Lesson Link #3 by writing stories about their dreams.

Grades 4–10

Kira-Kira by Cynthia Kadohata (2004) demonstrates to students that they have many opportunities in their lives that they can seize. Have students complete Lesson Link #3 and share their responses with a classmate and then report each other's answers to the class.

To accomplish great things, we must not only act, but also dream, not only plan, but also believe.

—Anatole France

THIS QUOTE MAKES ME THINK ABOUT . . .

PROMPTING TEACHERS' DEEPER THINKING

- How can you put your plans into action and reach your goals more rapidly? Can you reach more goals if you share them with your students, set a time aside each day for you and your students to work toward them, or allow students to work on specific, smaller objectives so that you can focus on the larger ones?
- What great dreams have you actualized in your professional life these past five years, and how have you accomplished them?
- Do you believe in yourself? Why?

LESSON LINKS

1. Ask students if they discuss their dreams with others or give opportunities for others to reveal their dreams.
2. Ask students how they act on their dreams.
3. Discuss the plans they make so a dream can come true.

LITERATURE LINKS

Grades K–4

Waiting for Wings by Lois Ehlert (2001) shows young children that if they have patience, they can attain many objectives. Ask students what dreams they have. Have students write a list of their dreams.

Grades 4–10

100 Photographs that Changed the World by Editors of Life Magazine (2003) is a collection of the most important photographs in the history of mankind. Each picture is followed by a description of how courageous people took important actions to maximize the opportunity depicted in each photograph to improve humanity. This is a great book for students who have difficulty maintaining the inspiration to maximize an opportunity. After they read this inspiring book, have students complete Lesson Link #3.

66 *It is not the critic who counts; not the man who points out how the strong man stumbles, or where the doer of deeds could have done them better. The credit belongs to the man who is actually in the arena, whose face is marred by dust and sweat and blood, who strives valiantly; who errs and comes short again and again . . . and who at the worst, if he fails, at least he fails while daring greatly.* **99**

— Theodore Roosevelt

THIS QUOTE MAKES ME THINK ABOUT . . .

PROMPTING TEACHERS' DEEPER THINKING

- Are you working to maximize the good that can be accomplished in a situation, or do you find yourself pointing out errors that others have made?
- Do you strive valiantly? How?
- What do you dare not do? Why?

LESSON LINKS

1. Ask students if and how they challenge themselves to take opportunities to improve situations, rather than sitting back and criticizing.

2. Discuss with students situations in which they have taken actions to improve things. What aspects of their character had to be exercised to do so? What were the effects of their actions on themselves and others?

3. Ask students if they believe in their abilities and courage to stand up against the status quo. Have them explain their answers.

LITERATURE LINKS

Grades K–4

The Puffins Are Back! by Gail Gibbons (1991) is a story about how we can all use opportunities every day, and reminds students that other living creatures depend on humans for their survival. Ask students to draw a picture of a hero or a creature they think represents bravery.

Grades 4–10

Who Moved My Cheese? for Teens: An A-Mazing Way to Change and Win! by Spencer Johnson (2002) helps teenagers understand other people, including those who are resistant to change for many different reasons. It can help them know how to deal with difficult decisions. Have students write in their journals about why it takes bravery to be a teenager.

Great is the art of beginning, but greater is the art of ending.

—Henry Wadsworth Longfellow

THIS QUOTE MAKES ME THINK ABOUT . . .

PROMPTING TEACHERS' DEEPER THINKING

- How do you feel when you complete a new initiative that you conceived?
- Think of a time in which you had difficulty realizing the benefits that originally presented themselves in a new professional opportunity. What caused the disillusionment you felt? What did you have to do to rescue the opportunity from turning into a professional problem? What did you learn about your ability to succeed when new opportunities appear?
- What is scary to you at the beginning of the school year? What have you learned from the quotations in this chapter that can assist you in viewing opportunities at the opening of the school year more positively?

LESSON LINKS

1. Ask students what they and their friends do at the end of a unit grading period or school year to celebrate.
2. Ask students if they get nervous at the beginning of every school year. Discuss how the quotations in this chapter can assist them to overcome this nervousness in the future.
3. Discuss with students whether they miss being in school during the summer or winter breaks, and how they can create learning opportunities during these hiatuses.

LITERATURE LINKS

Grades K–4

Nights of the Pufflings by Bruce McMillan (1995) shows students that when they act when an opportunity arises, they can make a difference in the world. Ask the following questions about this book: Was there a plan in this story, what was the plan, and was it successful? Ask students to respond in a class discussion.

Grades 4–10

Among the Hidden by Margaret Peterson Haddix (2000) is a great book to show students a model character who does not take things lying down. Ask students whether they enjoy standing up for what is right, and if so, why. Have them respond to these two questions with a partner and discuss what they liked about the ending of this story.

If we did things we are capable of we would astound ourselves.

—Thomas Edison

THIS QUOTE MAKES ME THINK ABOUT . . .

PROMPTING TEACHERS' DEEPER THINKING

- If you could become all that you want to become as a professional, how would your daily activities be different? Why?
- What do you think you're capable of?
- What do you think you are not capable of? Who told you and how can you overcome your self-imposed limitations?

LESSON LINKS

1. Ask your students to write about an opportunity they would like to have so they could actualize talents that they have not had the opportunity to employ as much as they desire.

2. Ask students if they think they have limited their capabilities through negative self-talk. Have them explain.

3. Ask students what will keep them from succeeding. Have them describe a time when they were surprised at how successful they were in learning (or accomplishing) something. What did they learn from that experience that could help their peers to exercise more of their capabilities in difficult situations?

LITERATURE LINKS

Grades K–4

Chasing Redbird by Sharon Creech (1998) is an enjoyable book filled with mysteries, dramas, suspense, and adventures. After they read this book, have students list five other books they plan on reading in the next month. Ask students how they think they can use books to expand their opportunities in life.

Grades 4–10

Journey to Jo'burg: A South African Story by Beverly Naidoo and Eric Velasquez (1988) describes apartheid and the challenges that existed during this time. The book shows how one family endures the suffering by expanding their opportunities. Have students discuss in groups what the goals were for this family and then report to the class.

God gives people every opportunity to make the right choice.

—Dr. James Dobson

THIS QUOTE MAKES ME THINK ABOUT . . .

PROMPTING TEACHERS' DEEPER THINKING

- What do you do to ensure that you make the best choices every day?
- What are your most difficult professional choices, and how can others assist you to make the right choices more often?
- Do you make the best choices for your students and for you? Do the teachers at your school make the best choices as a faculty for your students?

LESSON LINKS

1. Ask students how they tell if someone is making a good choice or a bad choice.
2. Do they tell their friends when they make a good or bad choice? Why or why not?
3. Ask students about the choices they made today.

LITERATURE LINKS

Grades K–4

Everything on a Waffle by Polly Horvath (2001) tells a story in a fun way about an orphanage and how the characters use their opportunities to create good and to not create good. Ask students what bad and good choices were made in this story. Have students create a list and compare their choices in groups or as a class.

Grades 4–10

Chain of Fire by Beverly Naidoo and Eric Velasquez (1989) is another great story for students in which the characters model determination and willpower. Ask students to analyze the choices that the main characters had to make in this story. Have students respond to Lesson Link #3 in a class discussion.

Excellence is an art. . . . We are what we repeatedly do. Excellence, then, is not an act, but a habit.

—Aristotle

THIS QUOTE MAKES ME THINK ABOUT . . .

PROMPTING TEACHERS' DEEPER THINKING

- What does excellence mean to you? Why?
- What habits do you have that contribute to or detract from your excellence as an educator?
- How can you make excellence a habit? What daily actions can you take?

LESSON LINKS

1. Have students write about their study and work habits that contribute to or detract from their excellence as lifelong learners.
2. Ask students to discuss the good or bad habits they have in school and at home.
3. Ask them if they think it is hard to break a bad habit. What habits would be hard for them to break? What kinds of support can they use to help them break these habits?

LITERATURE LINKS

Grades K–4

Coming On Home Soon by Jacqueline Woodson (2004) helps students learn how important it is to use every opportunity to read as much as they can about a wide variety of topics. Ask students why is it important to know how to read. Have them write responses down in journals.

Grades 4–10

Waiting for the Rain by Sheila Gordon (1996) describes how the main characters used opportunities in their lives to face the issues related to discrimination in South Africa. Ask students if they think it is hard for people who discriminate to stop. Discuss why and complete Lesson Link #3 in groups.

Give to us clear vision that we may know where to stand and what to stand for.

—Peter Marshall

THIS QUOTE MAKES ME THINK ABOUT . . .

PROMPTING TEACHERS' DEEPER THINKING

- Do you stand up for education and for students? Why or why not?
- What do you stand for?
- What do you do when students in a class put down a classmate?

LESSON LINKS

1. Ask students how they encourage their friends to stand up for themselves and what they believe in.
2. Ask students if they stick up for people who are made fun of.
3. Discuss with students the things they stand up for.

LITERATURE LINKS

Grades K–4

Ellington Was Not a Street by Ntozake Shange and Kadir Nelson (2004) is a book that you can read aloud for young students so that they can learn how this important American hero capitalized on his opportunities. Have students try to write a similar poem that describes how they have used the opportunities in their lives.

Grades 4–10

The Last Treasure by Janet Anderson (2003) is a book about bravery, strength, and the importance of relationships. It will remind students that their relationships and the opportunities they create with their family and friends help make them who they are and get them where they want to be. Have students respond to Lesson Link #3 in journals.

CLOSING REFLECTIONS

Quotes That Inspire You to Expand Your Opportunity

A Reflection on My Personal Literacy Goals

Use this space to write a reflection on the goals you have achieved or positive actions you have taken related to literacy or reading.

My Reading Success Story

Use this space to document any of your reading success stories.

THEMED COLLECTION 6 BOOK LIST

Anderson, J. (2003). *The Last Treasure.* London: Penguin.

Attenborough, L. (compiler). (2001). *Poetry by Heart.* New York: Scholastic.

Creech, S. (1998). *Chasing Redbird.* New York: HarperTrophy.

Crist, J. (2004). *What to Do When You're Scared and Worrie*d: *A Guide for Kids.* Minneapolis, MN: Free Spirit Publishing.

Editors of Life Magazine. (2003). *100 Photographs that Changed the World.* New York: Time Life Books.

Ehlert, L. (2001). *Waiting for Wings.* San Diego, CA: Harcourt Children's Books.

Gerety, E. (2003). *Combinations: Opening the Door to Student Leadership.* Washington DC: Whaleback Publishing.

Gibbons, G. (1991). *The Puffins Are Back!* New York: HarperCollins.

Gordon, S. (1996). *Waiting for the Rain.* New York: Random House.

Haddix, M. (2000). *Among the Hidden.* New York: Simon & Schuster.

Hendricks, H. (2003). *Teaching to Change Lives: Seven Proven Ways to Make Your Teaching Come Alive.* Sisters, OR: Multnomah.

Horvath, P. (2001). *Everything on a Waffle.* New York: Farrar, Straus and Giroux.

Johnson, S. (2002). *Who Moved My Cheese? for Teens: An A-Mazing Way to Change and Win!* London: Penguin.

Kadohata, C. (2004). *Kira-Kira.* New York: Atheneum.

McCutcheon, R. (1997). *Get Off My Brain: A Survival Guide for Lazy Students.* Minneapolis, MN: Free Spirit.

McMillan, B. (1995). *Nights of the Pufflings.* Boston: Houghton Mifflin.

Naidoo, B., & Velasquez, E. (1988). *Journey to Jo'burg: A South African Story.* New York: HarperTrophy.

Naidoo, B., & Velasquez, E. (1989). *Chain of Fire.* New York: HarperTrophy.

Osborne, M., & Murdocca, S. (2005). *Carnival at Candlelight.* New York: Random House.

Shange, N., & Nelson, K. (2004). *Ellington Was Not a Street.* New York: Simon & Schuster.

Wisniewski, D. (1999). *Tough Cookie.* New York: Lothrop, Lee, & Shepard.

Woodson, J. (2004). *Coming On Home Soon.* London: Penguin.

Themed Collection 7

Thinking to Obtain Meaning

Cathy Collins Block and Cinnamon S. Whiteley

READING SUCCESS STORY

The Importance of Thinking to Obtain Meaning

I was very lucky when I was growing up because I always enjoyed reading. I would not only read books, but I would also read the list of vocabulary words in the Reader's Digest *and test myself to see if I could get the definitions right. I still do that. I would do puzzle books and search wordbooks, just to learn new words (and still do). I encourage my kids and grandkids to do that too, and they know that I always have puzzle books and search wordbooks just waiting for them to work on.*

But today I still see children that not only don't like to read but they don't understand what they just read. Reading needs to be fun. I believe that if children enjoy reading, they will not only understand what they are reading but want to read more books.

—Rachel Escamilla, Volunteer in Children's Reading Program

PERSONAL LITERACY GOALS

Use this space to identify three goals or positive actions you would like to focus on related to thinking to obtain meaning that students can learn about during reading instruction and reading engagements.

To doubt everything and to believe everything are two equally convenient solutions; both dispense with the necessity of reflection.

—Henri Poincare

THIS QUOTE MAKES ME THINK ABOUT . . .

PROMPTING TEACHERS' DEEPER THINKING

- Have there been examples in your life when you have doubted everything or believed everything about a particular topic? How did you change your reaction?
- Do you think reflection is necessary as a teacher? Why? In what situations?
- What are ways in which you encourage your students to doubt?

LESSON LINKS

1. Ask students about the purpose of reflection.
2. Ask them if they have ever doubted something an adult told them. Have them explain what happened.
3. Ask students what machinery or equipment they use every day that they think people once laughed at when it was first invented.

LITERATURE LINKS

Grades K–4

Inventions No One Mentions by Chip Lovitt (1987) summarizes short stories of inventions that range from the comical to the strange. But as Lovitt points out with humorous quotes from the naysayers, many inventions were not well received when they were first introduced. This makes a nice companion reading for a science unit on simple machines. Have students respond to Lesson Link #3 in journals or in small groups and report to the class.

Grades 4–10

Unsolved Mysteries of American History (2000) and *More Unsolved Mysteries of American History* (2004), both by Paul Aron, offer facts about several mysteries in the past that remain unsolved, such as who was responsible for various battles and if Amelia Earhart was a spy. You can use these unsolved dilemmas to foster discussion and reflection. Have students respond to Lesson Link #2 at the conclusion of reading this book.

There are obviously two educations. One should teach us how to make a living. The other should teach us how to live.

—J. T. Adams

THIS QUOTE MAKES ME THINK ABOUT . . .

PROMPTING TEACHERS' DEEPER THINKING

- How do you feel about these two educations?
- Do you teach your students manners or other skills that are nonacademic? What are they?
- Do you believe in the education system in place today? How can you improve it in your own classroom?

LESSON LINKS

1. Ask students what kind of education they think they should receive.
2. Ask them what they would like to learn about and why. Do they enjoy learning life lessons from books?
3. Discuss with students whether they value their education.

LITERATURE LINKS

Grades K–4

Dragon Rider by Cornelia Funke (2004) is an adventurous story for elementary students seeking a journey to the world of imagination and discovery. Students can write about an adventure of their own after reading this book.

Grades 4–10

Chasing Vermeer by Blue Balliet (2004) is a mystery that challenges young minds to a greater extent than most books. Students will surely read this book to the end. Have students respond to Lesson Link #2 in their journals.

The purpose of life is to be happy, to matter, to be productive, to be useful, to have it make a difference that you lived at all.

—Leo Rosten

THIS QUOTE MAKES ME THINK ABOUT . . .

PROMPTING TEACHERS' DEEPER THINKING

- Do you feel that you are fulfilling a purpose when you are teaching?
- What is your purpose?
- Do you think you make a difference? How do you make a difference?

LESSON LINKS

1. Discuss with students their feelings about the purpose of life.

2. Ask students if they make a difference in the lives of others. Have them explain.

3. Ask students if they live their lives with a goal in mind. What does it mean to be productive and useful?

LITERATURE LINKS

Grades K–4

What Do You Do With a Tail Like This? by Robin Page and Steve Jenkins (2003) is a book for young students who love to learn interesting facts about animals. This picture book is great for many activities and can be used for collaborative assignments. Ask students to draw a jungle and assign a different animal to each student. Then ask students to research that animal and create a poster to introduce it.

Grades 4–10

The Perks of Being a Wallflower by Stephen Chbosky (1999) is most appropriate for the high school level. It is a story that teenagers will be able to relate to and find meaning in. After reading the story students can write about Lesson Link #2 in a writing assignment.

Bringing up father—when I was a boy of 14, my father was so ignorant I could hardly stand to have the old man around. But when I got to be 21, I was astonished at how much the old man had learned in seven years. 99

—Mark Twain

THIS QUOTE MAKES ME THINK ABOUT . . .

PROMPTING TEACHERS' DEEPER THINKING

- Do you try to learn from your students? How?
- How can you become more sensitive to students' needs?
- What have you learned from teaching?

LESSON LINKS

1. Ask students what they have learned this year.
2. Ask them if they are open to new ideas.
3. Ask students when and if they believe a person ever stops learning.

LITERATURE LINKS

Grades K–4

Bear Snores On by Karma Wilson and Jane Chapman (2002) is another book filled with illustrations and a story that is sure to be read over and over. Children will love the story line and this book is a great read when you have a few extra minutes. Ask your students to respond to Lesson Link #1 in their journals.

Grades 4–10

Speak by Laurie Halse Anderson (2001) is a novel for older readers. The book deals with issues that many children deal with on a daily basis, for example peer pressure. This is an excellent social story for discussing values and principles. Ask your students to discuss Lesson Link #2 with a partner and to come up with suggestions on how to be more open to other points of view.

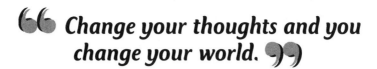

Change your thoughts and you change your world.

—Norman Vincent Peale

THIS QUOTE MAKES ME THINK ABOUT . . .

PROMPTING TEACHERS' DEEPER THINKING

- How do you change your students' lives?
- Do you change the lives of others in the community? How?
- Do you usually think positively or negatively? Why?

LESSON LINKS

1. Ask students how they change their world.

2. Discuss with students whether they think of the glass as half full or half empty.

3. Ask students whether they consider themselves positive or negative persons, and why.

LITERATURE LINKS

Grades K–4

Golem by David Wisniewski (1996) is a story with impressive illustrations that touches on history and an old Jewish legend. The story line of the mistreatment of people is an excellent starting off point for a discussion on how people should be treated and why.

Grades 4–10

Loser by Jerry Spinelli (2003) is a laugh-out-loud for readers who are in need of a lighthearted reading assignment. Have students respond to Lesson Link #2 as a journal entry.

With regard to excellence, it is not enough to know, but we must also try to put that knowledge to use.

—Aristotle

THIS QUOTE MAKES ME THINK ABOUT . . .

PROMPTING TEACHERS' DEEPER THINKING

- What does knowledge mean to you?
- Do you put what you have learned from workshops and conferences to use?
- What does excellence mean to you? Why?

LESSON LINKS

1. Ask students how they best apply new knowledge: Do they think about how they will apply the new knowledge while they are learning it? Do they talk about it, write about it, or observe others using it? Once they have answered this question about their best learning modality(ies), have them discuss how they can use what they have learned to increase the amount of new knowledge that they can apply to their lives in the future.

2. Ask them if they know how to apply new knowledge to their lives immediately after they learn it. If they do not, ask classmates to explain how they learn to use new information in their lives.

3. Ask students if they put what they know to use.

LITERATURE LINKS

Grades K–4

House for a Hermit Crab by Eric Carle (1991) shows students experiencing change in their lives how to deal with change. Have students discuss their feelings and describe how they try to understand change so they can focus on other things.

Grades 4–10

Silver Is for Secrets by Laurie Faria Stolarz (2005) is part of a series that many teenagers can relate to; it deals with issues that many teenagers analyze and try to find meaning from. Ask students to respond to Lesson Link #1 in pairs for a few minutes; then ask for volunteers to share their responses.

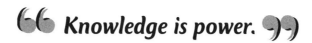 *Knowledge is power.*

—Francis Bacon

THIS QUOTE MAKES ME THINK ABOUT . . .

PROMPTING TEACHERS' DEEPER THINKING

- Why is knowledge powerful?
- What else is powerful?
- What does knowledge do for us?

LESSON LINKS

1. Ask students if they have known someone who was so knowledgeable that this person appeared to have a lot of power over situations and people.

2. Ask students if they think knowledge will make them successful. If so, how? If not, why not?

3. As a class, discuss the meaning of power.

LITERATURE LINKS

Grades K–4

The Three Pigs by David Wiesner (2001) is the newest version of the old tale of the three little pigs. Find the original book and compare the two books in a class discussion. Do you think your students have gained the knowledge they need for comparing and contrasting?

Grades 4–10

Spring (Witch Season) by Jeff Mariotte (2005) is a book for older readers who love suspense. It is an excellent example for older writers of what elements need to be in place for a story to be a page-turner. Students can list the elements in a story that are important for a book to be powerful. After completing the list, students can respond to Lesson Link #1 in an essay.

The one exclusive sign of thorough knowledge is the ability to teach.

—Aristotle

THIS QUOTE MAKES ME THINK ABOUT . . .

PROMPTING TEACHERS' DEEPER THINKING

- How do you acquire thorough knowledge?
- What abilities does one need to teach? Why?
- Can you give students more opportunities to demonstrate their knowledge by asking them to teach each other?

LESSON LINKS

1. Ask students what they do when they have to discuss or write about a topic they do not know a lot about.
2. Have students discuss how they prepare for a test.
3. Ask students how they feel after they help a friend who is having trouble with a homework or class assignment.

LITERATURE LINKS

Grades K–4

I Like Myself! by Karen Beaumont (2004) is a book about a young girl's unique identity. It is a great way to begin a discussion or a writing assignment on who you are and what you like about yourself. After they read this book, have students respond to Lesson Link #3 above by telling the class everything they learned about helping their friends.

Grades 4–10

Don't Die, Dragonfly by Linda Joy Singleton (2004) is the first in a series. The mystery is intriguing and even has a moral for readers. Students can summarize their response to Lesson Link #3 in a journal entry.

The world is but canvas to our imagination.

—Henry David Thoreau

THIS QUOTE MAKES ME THINK ABOUT . . .

PROMPTING TEACHERS' DEEPER THINKING

- Do you still use your imagination?
- Do you enjoy being creative? How can you increase your creativity?
- Do you allow your students to be imaginative in their assignments?

LESSON LINKS

1. Ask students what imagination means to them.
2. Ask students if they consider themselves creative. Why or why not?
3. Discuss the meaning of the word *creative* with students.

LITERATURE LINKS

Grades K–4

What Are YOU So Grumpy About? by Tom Lichtenheld (2003) pokes fun at grumpiness and is a laugh for all looking to find meaning in why they are angry. Have students use their imagination to create a skit of a time when they were grumpy.

Grades 4–10

Last Dance by Linda Joy Singleton (2005) is the second in the series mentioned above. The entire series is great for use in a unit on literature or writing. Ask students to define imagination and to list professions where people need to be creative in their jobs.

Two roads diverged in a wood and I—
I took the one less traveled by,
and that has made all the difference. 🙶🙶

—Robert Frost

THIS QUOTE MAKES ME THINK ABOUT . . .

PROMPTING TEACHERS' DEEPER THINKING

- What choices have you made that affected your life significantly?
- Which road for you was less traveled?
- What have you done recently that made all the difference for you? Why did it make all the difference?

LESSON LINKS

1. Have students write about a time in their lives when they had to make a really tough decision.
2. Ask students which path they would take.
3. Ask students what they want to be when they grow up.

LITERATURE LINKS

Grades K–4

How I Became a Pirate by Melinda Long and David Shannon (2003) is a great read for a discussion on job occupations and the steps involved in entering different professions. In response to Lesson Link #3 have students draw pictures of what they want to be when they grow up.

Grades 4–10

Because of Winn-Dixie by Kate DiCamillo (2001) is a book that can be read and analyzed chapter by chapter without losing the students' interest. After reading a chapter have students decide on their own what choices the main character or characters had to make in the story.

> 66 *Learning should be a joy and full of excitement. It is life's greatest adventure; it is an illustrated excursion into the minds of noble and learned men, not a conducted tour through a jail.* 99
>
> —Taylor Caldwell

THIS QUOTE MAKES ME THINK ABOUT . . .

PROMPTING TEACHERS' DEEPER THINKING

- What do you consider your life's greatest adventure?
- Is teaching and learning a joy to you?
- Do you think teaching is noble? Why?

LESSON LINKS

1. Discuss with your students the importance and value of learning. Ask them what lessons they have learned about getting older.
2. Have students write about whether learning is hard or easy for them.
3. Ask students what subjects they enjoy learning and have them explain.

LITERATURE LINKS

Grades K–4

The Man Who Walked Between The Towers by Mordicai Gerstein (2003) is a delight for young readers. It will give students a greater understanding of how words can help create a picture in their minds. Ask them what they consider hard about learning. Have students respond to this question in journals.

Grades 4–10

Best Foot Forward by Jane Bauer (2005) is a novel with many messages for readers. The writer reviews adolescence with the thought that we all get through it and that it is a part of life. Have students respond to Lesson Link #1 in groups and to create a poster or perform a skit in response to the question.

CLOSING REFLECTIONS

Quotes That Inspire You to Use Thinking to Obtain Meaning

A Reflection on My Personal Literacy Goals

Use this space to write a reflection on the goals you have achieved or positive actions you have taken related to literacy or reading.

My Reading Success Story

Use this space to document any of your reading success stories.

THEMED COLLECTION 7 BOOK LIST

Anderson, L. (2001). *Speak.* London: Penguin.
Aron, P. (2000). *Unsolved Mysteries of American History.* Hoboken, NJ: Wiley.
Aron, P. (2004). *More Unsolved Mysteries of American History.* Hoboken: NJ: Wiley.
Balliet, B. (2004). *Chasing Vermeer.* New York: Scholastic.
Bauer, J. (2005). *Best Foot Forward.* London: Penguin.
Beaumont, K. (2004). *I Like Myself!* San Diego, CA: Harcourt Children's Books.
Carle, E. (1991). *House for a Hermit Crab.* New York: Simon & Schuster.
Chbosky, S. (1999). *The Perks of Being a Wallflower.* New York: Simon & Schuster.
DiCamillo, K. (2001). *Because of Winn-Dixie.* Cambridge, MA: Candlewick Press.
Funke, C. (2004). *Dragon Rider.* Somerset, UK: The Chicken House.
Gerstein, M. (2003). *The Man Who Walked Between The Towers.* Hampshire, UK: Macmillan.
Lichtenheld, T. (2003). *What Are YOU So Grumpy About?* New York: Little, Brown.
Long, M., & Shannon, D. (2003). *How I Became a Pirate.* San Diego, CA: Harcourt Children's Books.
Lovitt, C. (1987). *Inventions No One Mentions.* New York: Scholastic.
Mariotte, J. (2005). *Spring (Witch Season).* New York: Simon & Schuster.
Page, R., & Jenkins, S. (2003). *What Do You Do With a Tail Like This?* Boston: Houghton Mifflin.
Singleton, L. (2004). *Don't Die, Dragonfly.* St. Paul, MN: Llewellyn.
Singleton, L. (2005). *Last Dance.* St. Paul MN, Llewellyn.
Spinelli, J. (2003). *Loser.* New York: HarperTrophy.
Stolarz, L. (2005). *Silver Is for Secrets.* St. Paul, MN: Llewellyn.
Wiesner, D. (2001). *The Three Pigs.* Boston: Houghton Mifflin.
Wilson, K., & Chapman, J. (2002). *Bear Snores On.* New York: Simon & Schuster.
Wisniewski, D. (1996). *Golem.* Boston: Houghton Mifflin.

Themed Collection 8

Identifying Our Strengths

Cathy Collins Block and Cinnamon S. Whiteley

READING SUCCESS STORY

The Importance of Identifying Our Strengths

While helping Jessica, a sixth grader from Fort Worth, discover the excitement of reading, I realized that no one had ever spent time helping her discover the beauty of her strengths when it came to reading. In fact she had been told quite the contrary. Jessica was told that she was not a very good reader; this comment had a lasting effect on her. When I began to tutor her I was able to identify her strengths and help her to draw on those strengths. Discovering these strengths was a pivotal time in her little, underdeveloped reading life. Because she now has learned how to identify her strengths, Jessica can read with a gentle confidence that speaks volumes.

As illustrated by this example, I have learned one very important lesson: I need to recognize early in the year the strengths of my students. But more importantly, I want my students to develop an understanding of the importance of their own strengths and the strengths of their peers. Teaching a child to draw from their strengths builds self-confidence and self-worth. It is important to me that my students walk away from my classroom each year changed and confident about who they are as people, and secure in their strengths. An exemplary teacher can make this happen for each of his or her students.

—Nicole M. Caylor, Preservice Secondary Teacher

PERSONAL LITERACY GOALS

Use this space to identify three goals or positive actions you would like to focus on related to identifying your students' strengths and how they can learn about this during reading instruction and reading engagements.

You gain strength, courage, and confidence by every experience in which you really stop to look fear in the face. You must do the thing you cannot do. 🙰

—Eleanor Roosevelt

THIS QUOTE MAKES ME THINK ABOUT . . .

PROMPTING TEACHERS' DEEPER THINKING

- What strengths do you bring to teaching?
- Are you a confident teacher? Why or why not?
- Do you remember how scared you were on your first day as a teacher?

LESSON LINKS

1. Ask students what fears they have about talking in class.
2. Ask students if they have other fears. How do they try to overcome them using a strength that they know they have?
3. Discuss with students the things they feel they cannot do.

LITERATURE LINKS

Grades K–4

I Knew You Could: A Book for All the Stops in Your Life by Craig Dorfman and Cristina Ong (2004) is a book that helps children learn how to deal with the ups and downs of life. Complete Lesson Link #3 in a class discussion.

Grades 4–10

The Other Side of Truth by Beverly Naido (2003) portrays dynamite characters who reveal that we all have the strength we need to get through anything. Students can work on Lesson Link #2 in journals after reading this book.

Do your work with your whole heart and you will succeed—there is so little competition.

—Elbert Hubbard

THIS QUOTE MAKES ME THINK ABOUT . . .

PROMPTING TEACHERS' DEEPER THINKING

- Does competition keep you from reaching your goals?
- What competition exists in teaching?
- Do you have competition in your classroom?

LESSON LINKS

1. Ask students if they believe the quote. Do they think that they can achieve anything if they do it with heart?
2. As a class, discuss what success does to people.
3. Ask students if they think competition is healthy.

LITERATURE LINKS

Grades K–4

If I Were a Lion by Sarah Weeks (2004) gives children a look at how they can and need to take responsibility. This is an excellent book to use in discussing classroom rules and teacher expectations.

Grades 4–10

Harry Potter and the Order of the Phoenix by J. K. Rowling (2003) is one in a series of must-reads. In each book in the series, Harry, the main character, must show courage when facing the danger that awaits him. In a class discussion, have students discuss how Harry Potter uses his "whole heart" to succeed in this story.

God grant me the serenity to accept the things I cannot change, the courage to change the things I can, and the wisdom to distinguish the one from the other.

—Reinhold Niebuhr

THIS QUOTE MAKES ME THINK ABOUT . . .

PROMPTING TEACHERS' DEEPER THINKING

- How do you accept failure?
- Where do you get your courage?
- What does serenity mean to you and why?

LESSON LINKS

1. Ask students what they do to inspire themselves when they continue to fail at a subject or a skill.
2. Ask students what acceptance means to them.
3. Discuss as a class whether students believe people can change.

LITERATURE LINKS

Grades K–4

Dog Heaven by Cynthia Rylant (1995) is a book for children who are dealing with the loss of a dog or any pet. Have students write or draw a picture about what they do to recover from losing something important to them.

Grades 4–10

A Day's Work by Eve Bunting (1997) is a book that examines the value of honesty. In today's world students need to be aware of why honesty is important and why people choose to not be honest. Students can complete Lesson Link #2 in a journal entry after reading this book.

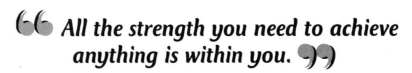

66 *All the strength you need to achieve anything is within you.* **99**

—Sara Henderson

THIS QUOTE MAKES ME THINK ABOUT . . .

PROMPTING TEACHERS' DEEPER THINKING

- Do you believe in yourself?
- Do your colleagues encourage you?
- How do you know when you have achieved something?

LESSON LINKS

1. Ask students how they know when they have achieved something.

2. Ask students where their strength comes from.

3. Have students describe someone that encourages them.

LITERATURE LINKS

Grades K–4

Season of the Sandstorms by Mary Pope Osborne (2005) is a good read for adventurous students. It is also an excellent book to read in conjunction with a geography lesson.

Grades 4–10

The Sisterhood of the Traveling Pants by Ann Brashares (2003) is a book that has adolescence written all over it. It is a fun read and reminds us of how important friendships are. Have students respond to Lesson Link #3 by listing people who encourage them and by working in groups to create a poster of encouraging words or phrases.

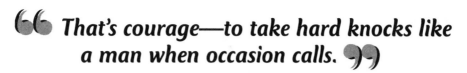

That's courage—to take hard knocks like a man when occasion calls.

—Plautus

THIS QUOTE MAKES ME THINK ABOUT . . .

PROMPTING TEACHERS' DEEPER THINKING

- Do you think it takes courage to be a teacher? Why?
- What is courage?
- Do you consider yourself courageous?

LESSON LINKS

1. Compliment your students' strengths.

2. Ask students if they criticize themselves.

3. Ask students if they consider themselves to be courageous people.

LITERATURE LINKS

Grades K–4

A Single Shard by Linda Sue Park (2003) deserves the awards it has received. This book is an excellent social story about friendships and the effect they have on us. Ask students to discuss Lesson Link #3 in pairs and then discuss with the class.

Grades 4–10

With Courage and Cloth: Winning the Fight for a Woman's Right to Vote by Ann Bausum (2004) is a powerful story that can be used in a history lesson and in a discussion on equality for all human beings.

Treat people as if they were what they ought to be, and you help them to become what they are capable of being.

—Johann Wolfgang von Goethe

THIS QUOTE MAKES ME THINK ABOUT . . .

PROMPTING TEACHERS' DEEPER THINKING

- Do you acknowledge your weaknesses? What are your weaknesses?
- How do you treat fellow teachers?
- How do you treat first-year teachers?

LESSON LINKS

1. Ask students if they treat all people the same. Why or why not?
2. Ask students what it feels like to be treated unfairly.
3. Have students write about whether they respect others who are different from them.

LITERATURE LINKS

Grades K–4

Through My Eyes by Ruby Bridges (1999) is an illustrated book about the courageous life of Ruby Bridges, written by herself. This book will show students that Ms. Bridges did not allow others to view her as less than she was. It will enable them to discover how they can see the best in all people.

Grades 4–10

Bud, Not Buddy by Christopher Paul Curtis (2002) is a read for those in need of hope. This book is full of emotions that students can relate to. Have students respond to Lesson Link #3 in a journal entry.

Our greatest glory is not in never falling, but in rising every time we fall.

—Confucius

THIS QUOTE MAKES ME THINK ABOUT . . .

PROMPTING TEACHERS' DEEPER THINKING

- Do you consider teaching glorious? Why?
- How do you overcome your failures?
- What do you consider failure? Why?

LESSON LINKS

1. Have students think about a time they failed at something but pulled themselves together and tried to go for it again. Ask them what motivated them.
2. What does it feel like when they fail?
3. What does it feel like to try again?

LITERATURE LINKS

Grades K–4

Stone Soup by Jon J. Muth (2003) is another version of a familiar folktale. The pages are filled with colorful pictures and insights that will lead to a discussion on different cultures. Have the students form in groups of 3–4 and assign each group a country they have never been to or know little about. Give them an assignment to learn three interesting things or facts about that country and report their findings to the class.

Grades 4–10

A Long Way From Chicago: A Novel in Stories by Richard Peck (2000) is a story that will be loved by all ages. The grandmother in the story comes off as harsh and critical but deep down she is soft and loving. This book can be used as a prompt for a journal entry or discussion on whether or not people choose to be mean and angry or are born that way.

I don't know what the key to success is but the key to failure is trying to please everyone.

—Bill Cosby

THIS QUOTE MAKES ME THINK ABOUT . . .

PROMPTING TEACHERS' DEEPER THINKING

- What do you think the key to success is?
- Do you please everyone? Why or why not?
- How else do people fail?

LESSON LINKS

1. Ask students how they ensure they will be successful.
2. Discuss whether success is important to your class.
3. Ask students if they are people-pleasers. Students can write about this on their own and then discuss their responses in pairs.

LITERATURE LINKS

Grades K–4

Old Turtle and the Broken Truth by Douglas Wood and Jon Muth (2003) is a story of how to accept other points of view and how to recognize the human spirit. After they read this book, have the class discuss Lesson Link #1 in groups.

Grades 4–10

Dreamland Lake by Richard Peck (2000) is a book that can be used to teach students about tone in literature and what writers consider when they are setting a tone for their story. It describes how authors rewrite every time their initial compositions fail to reach the clear communication that they desire. Discuss with students how they can use the lessons that Mr. Peck demonstrates in this book to build their abilities to respond to failures.

I am not bound to win, but I am bound to be true. I am not bound to succeed, but I am bound to live up to what light I have.

—Abraham Lincoln

THIS QUOTE MAKES ME THINK ABOUT . . .

PROMPTING TEACHERS' DEEPER THINKING

- What significant choices have you made that affected your life significantly?
- What are you living up to?
- Are you true to yourself?

LESSON LINKS

1. Have students write about a time in their lives when they had to make a really tough decision.
2. Ask students if they were true to themselves when they made this decision. How were they true to themselves?
3. Ask students what light they have.

LITERATURE LINKS

Grades K–4

The Trumpet of the Swan by E. B. White (2000) is a powerful story of a swan who is born unlike the rest of his family. Ask students to respond to Lesson Link #1 after finishing the story.

Grades 4–10

Charlotte's Web by E. B. White and Garth Williams (1952) is a must-read for every child. It touches our hearts and reminds us to appreciate the simple things in life. Have students discuss in groups what difficult decisions were made in this story and report their findings to the class.

CLOSING REFLECTIONS

Quotes That Inspire You to Identify Your Strengths

A Reflection on My Personal Literacy Goals

Use this space to write a reflection on the goals you have achieved or positive actions you have taken related to literacy or reading.

My Reading Success Story

Use this space to document any of your reading success stories.

THEMED COLLECTION 8 BOOK LIST

Bausum, A. (2004). *With Courage and Cloth: Winning the Fight for a Woman's Right to Vote.* Washington, DC: National Geographic.

Brashares, A. (2003). *The Sisterhood of the Traveling Pants.* New York: Random House.

Bridges, R. (1999). *Through My Eyes.* New York: Scholastic.

Bunting, E. (1997). *A Day's Work.* Boston: Houghton Mifflin.

Curtis, C. (2002). *Bud, Not Buddy.* New York: Random House.

Dorfman, C., & Ong, C. (2004). *I Knew You Could: A Book for All the Stops in Your Life.* New York: Scholastic.

Muth, J. (2003). *Stone Soup.* New York: Scholastic.

Naido, B. (2003). *The Other Side of Truth.* New York: HarperCollins.

Osborne, M. (2005). *Season of the Sandstorms.* New York: Random House.

Park, L. (2003). *A Single Shard.* New York: Random House.

Peck, R. (2000). *A Long Way From Chicago: A Novel in Stories.* London: Penguin.

Peck, R. (2000). *Dreamland Lake.* London: Penguin.

Rowling, J. (2003). *Harry Potter and the Order of the Phoenix.* New York: Arthur A. Scholastic.

Rylant, C. (1995). *Dog Heaven.* New York: Scholastic.

Weeks, S. (2004). *If I Were a Lion.* New York: Atheneum.

White, E. (2000). *The Trumpet of the Swan.* New York: HarperTrophy.

White, E., & Williams, G. (1952). *Charlotte's Web.* New York: HarperCollins.

Wood, D. & Muth J. (2003). *Old Turtle and the Broken Truth.* New York: Scholastic.

Themed Collection 9

Work, Study Skills, and Writing

Cathy Collins Block and Cinnamon S. Whiteley

READING SUCCESS STORY

The Importance of Work, Study Skills, and Writing

I find that no matter where I am working, whether it is at home or at school, I am constantly making lists. Lists for groceries, lists of ideas for future lesson plans, lists for what I need to remember to do or e-mails I need to write. To-do lists and general lists are an excellent tool for me to get organized and to be more efficient. My lists allowed for me to plan my time so that while I was taking a full course load of graduate classes and working full-time, I could still have time for myself and for my family and friends. I attribute part of my success and my ability to be organized to my to-do lists, a small and easy task that was introduced to me as a young girl in Zimbabwe. I still remember being in Mrs. Waldie's fourth-grade class and her showing the class how to create a to-do list where you checked off items as you completed them. Just as it was an amazing concept to me then, almost fifteen years later I continue to use that same model for many of my to-do lists.

In my first year of teaching I know that I will be introducing many organizational tools to my students to help them during the school year. As teachers we should share our secrets of success with our students. As a teacher I plan on bringing into my classroom part of what made me successful as a student in [earning] my undergraduate and graduate degree. No secrets of success should be hidden from our fellow staff members or from our students.

—Cinnamon S. Whiteley, Special Education Teacher

PERSONAL LITERACY GOALS

Use this space to identify three goals or positive actions you would like to focus on related to work, study skills, and writing that students can learn about this during reading instruction and reading engagements.

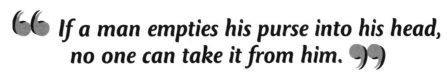

❝ *If a man empties his purse into his head,*
no one can take it from him. ❞

—Benjamin Franklin

THIS QUOTE MAKES ME THINK ABOUT . . .

PROMPTING TEACHERS' DEEPER THINKING

- How can you help students understand that no one can take their education from them, and that they can use what they read to change the future for themselves and others?
- Who is someone who helped you become more educated? What did you sacrifice to empty your purse into your head? Has it paid off?
- What is the most important action teachers with whom you work take to help each other empty their purses into your school and students? What does this reflection tell you about a new action you can take to increase the benefits of your personal readings and your reading instruction for your students?

LESSON LINKS

1. Ask students how they can use reading as a tool to invest in themselves. Have them write about a benefit they have already received from reading something in the past.

2. Ask students to describe a person that helped them to empty their purses into their heads so that no one could take their worth from them.

3. Ask students to explain how education and reading can help them throughout their lives in their desired professions, and invite adults to visit the class who are in professional roles to which students aspire. Ask the visitors to describe how they continued their education to advance their lives when they grew up.

LITERATURE LINKS

Grades K–4

The Teddy Bear by David McPhail (2002) shows students how one child's act of kindness "touched the future" of another person. Students can respond to Lesson Link #3 after reading this book as a class.

Grades 4–10

Lessons of a Century: A Nation's Schools Come of Age by the staff of Education Week (2000) outlines many discussions that students could have about the importance of education and investing in themselves throughout their lives. You could discuss each one separately, as each contains personal testimonials from famous people as to the value of education and reading in their lives, or you could divide students into teams that select a chapter of interest and report how the people in that chapter built time for reading and learning throughout their lives.

The wildly improbable happens every day.

—Rudolph Flesch

THIS QUOTE MAKES ME THINK ABOUT . . .

PROMPTING TEACHERS' DEEPER THINKING

- How do you prepare your class for the days you are absent?
- How do prepare for days when there is a pep rally or a presentation that breaks up your day?
- Do you explain to students what they need to do the day they return from an absence?

LESSON LINKS

1. Ask students how they handle returning to school after an absence.

2. Ask students how they prepare every day for school. How does each action contribute to their success in learning?

3. Have students write about whether they think that they can prepare for the happenings of every day life better by using the messages in the quotes from this and previous chapters in this book.

LITERATURE LINKS

Grades K–4

The Diary of a Worm by Doreen Cronin and Harry Bliss (2003) is a book that is written as a diary and is an excellent example for students who are learning to write journal entries. Have students respond to this story in a journal entry. Ask students, what did you learn from this story?

Grades 4–10

The Diary of Ma Yan: The Struggles and Hopes of a Chinese Schoolgirl by Ma Yan (2005) is the intriguing writing of a girl from a rural area in China. This diary is very truthful and is another excellent example of journal writing for an older group. Have students respond to the following question: What did you learn from this story?

Professionalism is knowing how to do it and when to do it, and then doing it.

—Frank Tyger

THIS QUOTE MAKES ME THINK ABOUT . . .

PROMPTING TEACHERS' DEEPER THINKING

- What do you do to prepare yourself for the school year during the summer or winter break?
- What does professionalism mean to you?
- Are you always professional at school and at workshops?

LESSON LINKS

1. Ask students if they view their teachers as professionals. Have them explain.
2. Ask students what jobs they consider to be professional jobs.
3. Ask students if they would conduct themselves in a more professional manner if their job were to go to school and learn.

LITERATURE LINKS

Grades K–4

Fame, Glory, and Other Things on My To-Do List by Janette Rallison (2005) is a humorous book about how things in life can go wrong. Have students create a to-do list for a week. At the end of the week, ask them if it helped them to get things done. Ask them what they liked and didn't like about a to-do list.

Grades 4–10

Study Skills for Life by L. Ron Hubbard (2000) is a guidebook for students with tips on better study habits and other helpful information to help a student academically. Have students respond to Lesson Link #3 in groups and have one person in each group record the responses and turn them in after the assignment is completed.

Time is what we want most,
but what we use worst. 99

—William Penn

THIS QUOTE MAKES ME THINK ABOUT . . .

PROMPTING TEACHERS' DEEPER THINKING

- Do you succeed with time management? What is your most successful strategy to manage your time that you could share with your colleagues?
- Do you think time fixes problems? Why?
- What kind of organization system do you use to manage your time?

LESSON LINKS

1. Ask students how they manage their class time.
2. Ask students if they are habitually late or early.
3. Have students write about whether they spend their time wisely.

LITERATURE LINKS

Grades K–4

Reader Rabbit 1st Grade Workbook published by Learning Company Books (2003) is one in a series of workbooks, divided by grade level, that help students with their academics. List the strategies or helpful hints from this book or another one from the series with your students. Do you think this list will be helpful?

Grades 4–10

Basic Study Manual by L. Ron Hubbard (2004) provides helpful reminders in how to study. Teachers can review these strategies to teach students how to study. Have students list the steps they go through when they study. Have students compare their lists to the other lists made by fellow students.

Life is like an onion, we peel off one layer at a time and sometimes we weep.

—Carl Sandburg

THIS QUOTE MAKES ME THINK ABOUT . . .

PROMPTING TEACHERS' DEEPER THINKING

- What significant changes has the passage of time created in your life, and how has the passage of time affected your life significantly?
- Do you agree or disagree with this quote?
- How is the passage of time like the pealing of an onion, especially when you cannot identify a solution for a difficult professional problem you face?

LESSON LINKS

1. Have students write about a time in their lives when they had to make a really tough decision.
2. Ask students what it feels like to make a tough decision.
3. In groups, have students create and act out a skit about a hard decision they had to make.

LITERATURE LINKS

Grades K–4

Oh, How I Wished I Could Read! by John Gile (1995) is a book to let students know the value of reading and how it plays a role in our everyday lives. Have students respond to Lesson Link #3 in groups after reading this book.

Grades 4–10

The Teenager's Guide to School Outside the Box by Rebecca Greene and Elizabeth Verdick (2000) is a guide to what students can be doing after school or on weekends, such as volunteering. Have students respond to Lesson Link #3 in groups after reading this book.

Great beginnings are not as important as the way one finishes.

—Dr. James Dobson

THIS QUOTE MAKES ME THINK ABOUT . . .

PROMPTING TEACHERS' DEEPER THINKING

- Do you feel good about yourself when you have completed a difficult professional task by using writing?
- What does it feel like to improve your profession through developing better work or study skills, or using writing?
- Do you celebrate special moments or occasions in your classroom by asking students to use writing, or to discuss how their work and study skills contributed to their successes?

LESSON LINKS

1. Ask students to write down their goals and explain how writing can assist them to grow throughout their lives.
2. Ask students if they show off when they win or are right.
3. Have students discuss whether they are good losers.

LITERATURE LINKS

Grades K–4

Stick Up for Yourself: Every Kid's Guide to Personal Power and Positive Self-Esteem by Gershen Kaufman, Lev Raphael, and Pamela Espeland (1999) empowers students to stand up for themselves. With your students, create a list of suggestions from this book for what they could do when they are bullied or teased.

Grades 4–10

Goal Setting for Students by John Bishop (2003) is an excellent book for students to refer to when writing out their goals and to help them understand the purpose of goal setting. Have students respond to Lesson Link #1 in a journal entry.

66 *What you do when you don't have to determines what you will be when you can no longer help it.* **99**

—Rudyard Kipling

THIS QUOTE MAKES ME THINK ABOUT . . .

PROMPTING TEACHERS' DEEPER THINKING

- What would you do if something kept you from teaching?
- How do you spend your weekends and breaks?
- What do you love doing? How can you build work skills and use writing in doing this task to increase your proficiencies in this area of interest?

LESSON LINKS

1. Ask students how they spend their summer and winter breaks and if they could add activities to improve their work skills, study skills, or writing abilities.

2. Have students make a list of things they love to do. Ask them how their work skills, study skills, and writing abilities have contributed to their proficiencies in these areas of interest.

3. Ask students what they would be upset about if they could no longer do the things they love, and how they can prepare now to limit the amount of loss they could experience in the future.

LITERATURE LINKS

Grades K–4

Milk to Ice Cream by Inez Snyder (2003) is a great book to teach students about lists, especially the purpose of grocery lists. Create a grocery list as a class for what one would need to get at the store in order make ice cream at home.

Grades 4–10

Crash by Jerry Spinelli (1996) is a book that describes what one seventh grader did to overcome the absence of something he did not have. Every student can read this book and then complete Literature Link 3, writing about whether they would follow the path Crash took or not.

*I long to accomplish a great and noble task,
but it is my chief duty to accomplish humble
tasks as if they were great and noble.* **99**

—Helen Keller

THIS QUOTE MAKES ME THINK ABOUT . . .

PROMPTING TEACHERS' DEEPER THINKING

- Do you consider it a great task or a humble task to teach?
- What is your chief duty?
- Have you completed a noble task in your life? What was it?

LESSON LINKS

1. Show your students how to organize their notes to help them review and study for a test or quiz.
2. Ask students what "noble" means to them.
3. Have students list the things they would like to have accomplished in ten years.

LITERATURE LINKS

Grades K–4

Did I Ever Tell You How Lucky You Are? by Dr. Seuss (1973) helps young students gain perspective on their good fortune. After reading this story, ask students to create a list of how lucky they are to have the things they have and to do the things they like to do.

Grades 4–10

Succeed Every Day: Daily Readings for Teens by Pamela Espeland (2000) is a book of daily quotes that can be used as an inspirational tool. Ask students to create their own quotes to inspire people.

Take time to deliberate, but when the time for action has arrived, stop thinking and go in.

—Napoleon Bonaparte

THIS QUOTE MAKES ME THINK ABOUT . . .

PROMPTING TEACHERS' DEEPER THINKING

- Do you live your life by your schedule?
- Do you have time for others in your life?
- Are you too busy to enjoy life?

LESSON LINKS

1. Ask students how they keep themselves on task.
2. Have students discuss in groups what they use to help manage their time.
3. Ask students if they make time for themselves.

LITERATURE LINKS

Grades K–4

The Traveler's Atlas: A Global Guide to the Places You Must See in a Lifetime by Chris Schuler and Geoffrey Roy (1998) is a great guidebook. It shows students pictures and facts about many places in the world. Assign groups and give each group a different country. Have students create a list of what they would need to pack to go to that country. They will need to consider the climate and the activities they will do on their trip.

Grades 4–10

The Ten Commandments of Goal Setting: Violate Them at Your Own Risk! by Gary Ryan Blair (1999) is a book that teaches students about goal setting and the value of having goals. Have students write out a time schedule for themselves to use for one full week, and then discuss as a class how the schedule was useful or how it was not useful.

I have always admired the ability to bite off more than one can chew and then chew it.

—William Dewille

THIS QUOTE MAKES ME THINK ABOUT . . .

PROMPTING TEACHERS' DEEPER THINKING

- Do you often bite off more than you can chew?
- Who do you admire? Why? How do they manage their time in a way that adds to their success?
- Can you learn to say no to unnecessary tasks by telling the person who asks you to do something that you already have a prior commitment for that time period or that you already have established a priority that will keep you from saying yes at this time?

LESSON LINKS

1. In pairs, have students discuss how they handle situations in which they have overcommitted themselves.
2. Ask students if they habitually overschedule themselves. Ask them to develop a list of responses that they can use when others ask them to do things that would cause them to be overscheduled.
3. Have students list things they do after school with their time, and ask how they can maximize their time commitments so that they can better achieve the goals that they most value.

LITERATURE LINKS

Grades K–4

Make Your Own Calendar 2006 by Steve Haskamp (2005) is a great guide for a calendar activity for any class. Students can create their own calendars and update them every Monday with new activities or projects that will be coming up in the week or in the month.

Grades 4–10

How to Do Homework Without Throwing Up by Trevor Romain and Elizabeth Verdick (1997) is a how-to on getting through homework. Students can discuss Lesson Link #3 after they have finished reading the book.

CLOSING REFLECTIONS

Quotes That Inspire You in Work, Study Skills, and Writing

A Reflection on My Personal Literacy Goals

Use this space to write a reflection on the goals you have achieved or positive actions you have taken related to literacy or reading.

My Reading Success Story

Use this space to document any of your reading success stories.

THEMED COLLECTION 9 BOOK LIST

Bishop, J. (2003). *Goal Setting for Students.* St Louis, MO: Accent on Success.

Blair, G. (1999). *The Ten Commandments of Goal Setting: Violate Them at Your Own Risk!* Syracuse, NY: Goalsguy Learning Systems.

Cronin, D., & Bliss, H. (2003). *Diary of a Worm.* New York: HarperCollins.

Espeland, P. (2000). *Succeed Every Day: Daily Readings for Teens.* Minneapolis, MN: Free Spirit.

Geisel, T. (Dr. Seuss). (1973). *Did I Ever Tell You How Lucky You Are?* New York: Random House.

Gile, J. (1995). *Oh, How I Wished I Could Read!* Rockford, IL: John Gile Communications.

Greene, R., & Verdick, E. (2000). *The Teenager's Guide to School Outside the Box.* Minneapolis, MN: Free Spirit.

Haskamp, S. (2005). *Make Your Own Calendar 2006.* New York: Little, Brown.

Hubbard, L. (2000). *Study Skills for Life.* St. Louis, MO: Effective Education.

Hubbard, L. (2004). *Basic Study Manual.* St. Louis, MO: Effective Education.

Kaufman, G., Raphael, L., & Espeland, P. (1999). *Stick Up for Yourself: Every Kid's Guide to Personal Power and Positive Self-Esteem.* Minneapolis, MN: Free Spirit.

McPhail, D. (2002). *The Teddy Bear.* New York: Henry Holt.

Rallison, J. (2005). *Fame, Glory, and Other Things on My To-Do List.* New York: Walker.

Reader Rabbit 1st Grade Workbook. (2003). San Francisco: Learning Company Books.

Romain, T., & Verdick, E. (1997). *How to Do Homework Without Throwing Up.* Minneapolis, MN: Free Spirit.

Schuler, C., & Roy, G. (1998). *The Traveler's Atlas: A Global Guide to the Places You Must See in a Lifetime.* Hauppauge, NY: Barron's Educational Series.

Snyder, I. (2003). *Milk to Ice Cream.* Danbury, CT: Children's Press.

Spinelli, J. (1996). *Crash.* New York: Scholastic.

Staff of *Education Week.* (2000). *Lessons of a Century: A Nation's Schools Come of Age.* Bethesda, MD: Editorial Projects in Education.

Yan, M. (2005). *The Diary of Ma Yan: The Struggles and Hopes of a Chinese Schoolgirl.* New York: HarperCollins.

Themed Collection 10

Literacy Worlds

Beth A. Earley,
Molly D. Dahl,
and Susan E. Israel

READING SUCCESS STORY

The Importance of Literacy Worlds

As a sixth-grade language arts teacher, I battle daily with keeping the attention of my students because they are interested in everything but language arts at this age. My main goal for students is to instill within them a love of reading. Throughout the first quarter of one year, I tried everything in my power to get an unmotivated boy to enjoy reading. He did not have a major problem with comprehension, or any other reading skills, but it was such a painful experience for him to sit and read that he was miserable every time he was given a reading assignment. He and I talked on a regular basis about his interests, and things going on in his life, but even books involving sports and racing did not keep his attention. At the end of the first quarter his grade was pretty low due to his lack of interest in reading. I decided to pull out the big gun, Where the Red Fern Grows *by Wilson Rawls.*

In my ten years of teaching this novel has been a favorite of almost all of my students. If this book doesn't change feelings about reading, nothing will. Normally we don't read this book until the end of the school year, but I was determined to motivate this boy, and prove to him that he could enjoy reading. As usual, he was reluctant to begin this book or even participate in the introductory activity. I decided that we would listen to the book on tape and follow along rather than read it aloud together. From the second I pushed play on the recorder, Luke was hooked. I don't know if it was the voice on the recording, the descriptive writing of Wilson Rawls, or the topic of hunting, but he was paying attention, asking questions, and bugging me on a daily basis to read the book. From that day on, he was a reader. Once he realized that there were books out there that interested him, he slowly developed a love of reading. I recently got an e-mail from him thanking me for a rewarding sixth-grade experience, and instilling in him a love of books. He had just finished watching the movie Where the Red Fern Grows *on TV and it reminded him of me. My student just finished his degree in political science and will be starting law school next fall.*

—Miss Mothersole, Sixth-Grade Teacher

PERSONAL LITERACY GOALS

Use this space to identify three goals or positive actions you would like to focus on related to literacy worlds and how students can learn about them during reading instruction and reading engagements.

66 *When I look back, I am so impressed again with the life-giving power of literature. If I were a young person today, trying to gain a sense of myself in the world, I would do that again by reading, just as I did when I was young.* **99**

—Maya Angelou

THIS QUOTE MAKES ME THINK ABOUT . . .

PROMPTING TEACHERS' DEEPER THINKING

- How did reading play a part in your life as a child?
- What advice would you give students about the joy of reading?
- What are some ways that you could possibly inspire young students to read?

LESSON LINKS

1. Ask students what their favorite books were when they were small children.

2. Ask students what characters they identify with most in all the books they have read.

3. Have students discuss some reasons that they read.

LITERATURE LINKS

Grades K–4

Here Comes the Strikeout by Leonard Kessler (1992) is a great book that celebrates over-coming adversity. After reading this book have students discuss the character they identified with most, as suggested in Lesson Link #2, and ask why.

Grades 4–10

The History of Counting by Denise Schmandt-Besserat (1999) shows students the history behind counting—from where it originated to why we do what we do now. Have children discuss whether mathematical books are among their favorites or not, as described in Lesson Link #1 above.

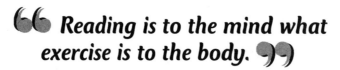

❝ *Reading is to the mind what exercise is to the body.* ❞

—Joseph Addison

THIS QUOTE MAKES ME THINK ABOUT . . .

PROMPTING TEACHERS' DEEPER THINKING

- Like exercise, reading is not something everyone wants to do. How can you make reading more appealing to the reluctant reader?
- How can you become more involved with reading and therefore a better model for students?
- How can you provide a more level playing field for all students learning to read in your classroom?

LESSON LINKS

1. Ask students why Joseph Addison would compare exercise to reading.
2. Have students describe one time when practice really did make perfect for them or someone else.
3. Ask students to describe one thing about reading that they would like to be better at. How can they get better at that?

LITERATURE LINKS

Grades K–4

Sideways Stories From Wayside School by Louis Sachar (1998) is a book that allows students to read in short spurts to help grab their attention. This book can be used before you complete Lesson Link #2 above.

Grades 4–10

Harry Potter and the Sorcerer's Stone by J. K. Rowling (1998) is a fantastic book that enables students to become a part of another world. This book can be used chapter by chapter to discuss Lesson Link #3 above.

It is not enough to simply teach children to read; we have to give them something worth reading. Something that will stretch their imaginations—something that will help them make sense of their own lives and encourage them to reach out toward people whose lives are quite different from their own. 🙶

—Katherine Patterson

THIS QUOTE MAKES ME THINK ABOUT . . .

PROMPTING TEACHERS' DEEPER THINKING

- What do you consider something worth reading for your students?
- How can you teach students about diversity and acceptance?
- What are some issues that you face regarding diversity in the classroom?

LESSON LINKS

1. Ask students how they approach someone who is different from themselves.
2. Have students write about a time when they thought someone was very different from themselves, only to find the person was not so different after all.
3. In groups, have students discuss a time when they felt out of place.

LITERATURE LINKS

Grades K–4

Stellaluna by Janell Cannon (1993) is a fantastic book about understanding and acceptance. This would be a great anticipatory set for a lesson on diversity and for Lesson Link #3.

Grades 4–10

Every Second Counts by Lance Armstrong (2003) is an amazing story of recovery and sheer determination. After reading this powerful story, students can begin working on Lesson Link #2.

A truly great book should be read in youth, again in maturity and once more in old age, as a fine building should be seen by morning light, at noon and by moonlight.

—Robertson Davies

THIS QUOTE MAKES ME THINK ABOUT . . .

PROMPTING TEACHERS' DEEPER THINKING

- How can you convince older children to read something more than once?
- When have you been in a situation where you saw something in a new light?
- What books did you read as a child that you think you should now read as an adult?

LESSON LINKS

1. Ask students why they think Robertson Davies believes you should reread books at different ages.
2. Have students write about a time they have seen something in a different light.
3. Ask students why it is that many people judge others on first impressions.

LITERATURE LINKS

Grades K–4

Alone in his Teacher's House by Louis Sachar (1994) helps demonstrate to students that there is more to a book than its cover. This book helps students see beyond their initial impressions. Ask children what they have learned from this book that could help them prepare a better answer for Lesson Link #2 above.

Grades 4–10

Tuck Everlasting by Natalie Babbitt (1985) is a great book to be read as a youngster and again as an adult. The book inspires deep thinking on moral issues and adds a value-packed lesson that asks students what they would do in this situation. Discuss with students what they have learned from the characters in this book that could create a better answer to Lesson Link #3 above.

Books are the quietest and most constant of friends; they are the most accessible and wisest of counselors, and the most patient of teachers.

—Charles W. Eliot

THIS QUOTE MAKES ME THINK ABOUT . . .

PROMPTING TEACHERS' DEEPER THINKING

- What types of books do you feel you learn the most from?
- How can reading assist you in becoming a more patient teacher?
- What characteristics make a book more or less interesting?

LESSON LINKS

1. Ask students what qualities in a book make it become their constant friend.
2. Ask students what book they could read over and over again. Have them explain.
3. Have students write about a time when they couldn't put a book down because it talked about a different kind of person, place, or life.

LITERATURE LINKS

Grades K–4

Doctor Desoto by William Steig (1986) is a great book about trusting your instincts. The lesson taught here is that you must always make sure you are OK before you can help others. After reading this book ask children to describe what qualities in the book enable it to become the "most constant of friends," as described in Lesson Link #1 above.

Grades 4–10

The House on Mango Street by Sandra Cisneros (1991) is a series of vignettes describing a young girl and her family who come into a new neighborhood and enter a world unlike one they have ever known. After reading this book ask students to list all the books they have read that they could not put down.

When we read a story, we inhabit it. The covers of the book are like a roof and four walls. What is to happen next will take place within the four walls of the story. And this is possible because the story's voice makes everything its own.

—John Berger

THIS QUOTE MAKES ME THINK ABOUT . . .

PROMPTING TEACHERS' DEEPER THINKING

- How do you teach students to inhabit books they are reading?
- How do you teach students to identify with the elements of story (character, plot, setting, etc.)?
- What influence do you have over children's reading within your four walls?

LESSON LINKS

1. Ask students if they have ever read a book in which the characters seemed alive like real people. Have them explain.
2. Ask students what John Berger means by "the story's voice."
3. Ask students why they think they like some books more than others.

LITERATURE LINKS

Grades K–4

Sarah, Plain and Tall by Patricia MacLachlan (1987) is a great book to show students the emotional pull of a story. After reading this book have students describe how the characters were created to seem as if they were real, as described in Lesson Link #1 above.

Grades 4–10

Holes by Louis Sachar (2000) is a book which pulls the reader in immediately. Students identify with the character because he is just like them. This book draws readers in because of the adventure and excitement of the story line. After they read this book have students describe how the characters were created to seem as if they were real as described in Lesson Link #1 above, and ask how the reader sees the world differently after reading the book.

Our high respect for a well-read person is praise enough for literature.

—Ralph Waldo Emerson

THIS QUOTE MAKES ME THINK ABOUT . . .

PROMPTING TEACHERS' DEEPER THINKING

- What does this quote mean to you?
- What are some strategies that you can teach your students that will help them become good readers?
- What are some characteristics of a well-read person?

LESSON LINKS

1. Ask students what characteristics they think a well-read person has.
2. Ask students if they consider themselves well-read. Have them explain.
3. Ask students why they think that well-read persons are highly respected.

LITERATURE LINKS

Grades K–4

Questions and Answers About Weather by M. Jean Craig (1996) is a great example of a non-fiction book with many interesting facts. By using books such as this one to learn about all different subject areas, students have a wider knowledge base to draw from when making connections to stories and building on their prior knowledge base. After they finish reading this book, ask students how the information they read could help them consider themselves to be better readers. Discuss Lesson Link #2 above.

Grades 4–10

Dragonwings by Lawrence Yep (1990) is about creating different opportunities by overcoming obstacles. This book teaches students to look beyond the negatives to get to the most positive outcomes. Ask students what they have learned from this book that will help them to become better readers or more respected persons as described in Lesson Link #3 above.

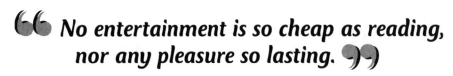

No entertainment is so cheap as reading, nor any pleasure so lasting.

—Lady M. W. Montague

THIS QUOTE MAKES ME THINK ABOUT . . .

PROMPTING TEACHERS' DEEPER THINKING

- How do you engage students in reading that will give them long-lasting pleasure?
- Think of the characteristics of a book that has had a lasting impression on you.
- How has a teacher in your past inspired you to read books?

LESSON LINKS

1. Ask students if they have ever read a book and then seen the movie, and found that the movie was not as good as the book. Have them explain.
2. Ask students why they would rather read a book than see a movie.
3. Ask students in what ways reading a book is entertaining.

LITERATURE LINKS

Grades K–4

Charlie and the Chocolate Factory by Roald Dahl (1998) is a great fantasy book that is extremely entertaining for children and adults of all ages. This has been a favorite story since its publication. There is a theme of greed which would be a wonderful opening for a discussion in the classroom about this topic. This book can be used with Lesson Link #1 above.

Grades 4–10

Freak the Mighty by Rodman Philbrick (2001) is an exceptional book that stirs up students' thinking. The author helps teach a wonderful lesson about overcoming adversity and learning to accept those who are different from you. This is a book that makes students think twice about teasing someone who is different than they are. It can be used with Lesson Link #3 above.

Books find not wisdom where none was before. But where some is, there reading makes it more.

—John Harington

THIS QUOTE MAKES ME THINK ABOUT . . .

PROMPTING TEACHERS' DEEPER THINKING

- As an educator, how do you select books that are rich in meaning?
- What types of books tend to be meaningful to students?
- What genres have the most wisdom-packed stories?

LESSON LINKS

1. Ask students about some of the lessons they have learned from reading books.
2. Have students write about a book that has taught them a life lesson and how they used that lesson.
3. Have students write their own stories that include a lesson or a moral.

LITERATURE LINKS

Grades K–4

If You Lived at the Time of the American Revolution by Kay Moore (1998) is an excellent non-fiction historical book. Students will find this book to be more interesting than a textbook in that they can get a sense for what it was like to live during this time. This is a fantastic book to help expand students' knowledge base in history. Ask children if this book taught them a lesson they can use in life.

Grades 4–10

Hatchet by Gary Paulsen (1999) is a wonderful adventure book to help inspire students to do things on their own. This story pulls in boys and girls on an emotional ride in which the main character, a child, survives alone in the wilderness. This book can be used with Lesson Link #3 above. Ask students to describe times when they grew wiser because they overcame an obstacle in their lives.

The more that you read, the more things you will know. The more that you learn, the more places you'll go.

—Dr. Seuss

THIS QUOTE MAKES ME THINK ABOUT . . .

PROMPTING TEACHERS' DEEPER THINKING

- How has reading benefited you in your career?
- If you could not read, how would that limit you in your life?
- How can you demonstrate to students the longevity of benefits that they will get from reading?

LESSON LINKS

1. Have students write about a time when they would have been in trouble if they hadn't been able to read.

2. Ask when reading has taken them to new places.

3. Ask what important things they learn from reading.

LITERATURE LINKS

Grades K–4

From the Mixed-Up Files of Mrs. Basil E. Frankweiler by E. L. Konigsburg (1998) is a book with a character struggling to become someone. This helps students see that they are not alone in their desire to stand out from the crowd. Pair this book with Lesson Link #1 above.

Grades 4–10

Roll of Thunder, Hear My Cry by Mildred Taylor (1991) is a great book demonstrating the overcoming of adversity. This story shows students that they can get places with a little persistence and strong will. It can be used with Lesson Link #1 above.

CLOSING REFLECTIONS

Quotes That Inspire You to Think Differently About Literacy Worlds

A Reflection on My Personal Literacy Goals

Use this space to write a reflection on the goals you have achieved or positive actions you have taken related to literacy or reading.

My Reading Success Story

Use this space to document any of your reading success stories.

THEMED COLLECTION 10 BOOK LIST

Armstrong, L. (2003). *Every Second Counts.* New York: Random House.

Babbitt, N. (1985). *Tuck Everlasting.* New York: Farrar, Strauss, and Giroux.

Cannon, J. (1993). *Stellaluna.* San Diego, CA: Harcourt Children's Books.

Cisneros, S. (1991). *The House on Mango Street.* New York: Random House.

Craig, M. (1996). *Questions and Answers About Weather.* New York: Scholastic.

Dahl, R. (1998). *Charlie and the Chocolate Factory.* London: Penguin.

Kessler, L. (1992). *Here Comes the Strikeout.* New York: HarperTrophy.

Konigsburg, E. (1998). *From the Mixed-Up Files of Mrs. Basil E. Frankweiler.* New York: Simon & Schuster.

MacLachlan, P. (1987). *Sarah, Plain and Tall.* New York: HarperTrophy.

Moore, K. (1998). *If You Lived at the Time of the American Revolution.* New York: Scholastic.

Paulsen, G. (1999). *Hatchet.* New York: Simon & Schuster.

Philbrick, R. (2001). *Freak the Mighty.* New York: Scholastic.

Rowling, J. (1998). *Harry Potter and the Sorcerer's Stone.* New York: Scholastic.

Sachar, L. (1994). *Alone in his Teacher's House.* New York: Random House.

Sachar, L. (1998). *Sideways Stories From Wayside School.* New York: HarperTrophy.

Sachar, L. (2000). *Holes.* New York: Random House.

Schmandt-Besserat, D. (1999). *The History of Counting.* New York: HarperCollins.

Steig, W. (1986). *Doctor Desoto.* New York: Scholastic.

Taylor, M. (1991). *Roll of Thunder, Hear My Cry.* London: Penguin.

Yep, L. (1990). *Dragonwings.* New York: Simon & Schuster.

Collaborative Communities at School and Home

Cathy Collins Block and Cinnamon S. Whiteley

READING SUCCESS STORY

The Importance of Collaborative Communities

I was amazed at what happened when we had teachers test this book's collection of quotes with their pupils. Several K–3 teachers picked quotes that I felt were too old for their children to comprehend. The student's responses were remarkable. They not only understood in their own way but gave me another perspective to consider. A lesson for all teachers: Don't underestimate the power of literacy. After all, it is for all mankind.

—JoAnn Zinke, Teacher of Adults and Children

PERSONAL LITERACY GOALS

Use this space to identify three goals or positive actions you would like to focus on related to collaborative communities and how students can learn about them during reading instruction and reading engagements.

Nine-tenths of education is encouragement.

—Anatole France

THIS QUOTE MAKES ME THINK ABOUT . . .

PROMPTING TEACHERS' DEEPER THINKING

- How often do you encourage your students during the day?
- Who encourages you every day?
- Do you need people to encourage you?

LESSON LINKS

1. Ask students what they say to their friends to encourage them.
2. Have students write about a time they encouraged a family member.
3. Ask students if they like or need encouragement from others.

LITERATURE LINKS

Grades K–4

On the Town: A Community Adventure by Judith Caseley (2002) is the story of a mother and child who walk around the town to complete errands. The child learns about his community and the people that play a part in it. Have students list various members of their community after reading this book.

Grades 4–10

If the World Were a Village: A Book About the World's People by David J. Smith (2002) is a book that teachers can use it to discuss history, math, and social studies. Ask students to write about Lesson Link #1 and to write one encouraging phrase and to try to translate it into another language. As a class, create a poster with these phrases.

It is the supreme art of the teacher to awaken joy in creative expression and knowledge.

—Albert Einstein

THIS QUOTE MAKES ME THINK ABOUT . . .

PROMPTING TEACHERS' DEEPER THINKING

- What joy do you get from working with parents and students together as a learning community?
- When parents come to your classroom to assist you in teaching, do you enjoy it? If not, how can you change those occasions so that everyone in the classroom enjoys and benefits from the times together?
- Are you an inclusive teacher?

LESSON LINKS

1. Ask students what they do to inspire themselves, their friends, and their family.
2. Have students write about whether they consider themselves creative or knowledgeable or both.
3. Ask students to ask their parents about their most enjoyable learning experiences. Have them share some of these stories in class.

LITERATURE LINKS

Grades K–4

Do Something in Your Community by Amanda Rondeau (2004) will be useful to discuss what people can do in their communities to make a difference. This book is a great lead to a discussion on people and their role in the community.

Grades 4–10

It's Disgusting and We Ate It! True Food Facts From Around the World and Throughout History by James Solheim (2001) is a book to get students discussing and intrigued about different cultures and the foods their people eat or consider to be delicacies. Have students write about Lesson Link #3 in their journals.

Education is not the filling of the pail, but the lighting of a fire.

—William Butler Yeats

THIS QUOTE MAKES ME THINK ABOUT . . .

PROMPTING TEACHERS' DEEPER THINKING

- How do you light a fire in your students?
- Who else inspires your students?
- What can you do to increase the frequency with which other adults visit your class to inspire your students and help them learn to read?

LESSON LINKS

1. Ask students what the quote means to them.
2. Ask who lights the fires of learning in them.
3. Ask them to write about a time a family member inspired them.

LITERATURE LINKS

Grades K–4

Our Community Garden by Barbara Pollak (2004) is a story of a group of people who work together on a community garden. Have students work on a project together where everyone contributes. One project could be a community library where students will donate a book or two to the school library.

Grades 4–10

Material World: A Global Family Portrait by Peter Menzel, Charles C. Mann, and Paul Kennedy (1995) will show students through photographs how other people live around the world. It also shows students about what people consider necessary to live. Ask students to respond to Lesson Link #3 by writing a letter thanking a member of their family who inspires them.

Most of us end up with no more than five or six people who remember us. Teachers have thousands of people who remember them for the rest of their lives.

—Andy Rooney

THIS QUOTE MAKES ME THINK ABOUT . . .

PROMPTING TEACHERS' DEEPER THINKING

- What choices have you made that affected people in your life significantly?
- Do you remember the good or the bad about people from your past?
- Do you think people remember the good or the bad about you?

LESSON LINKS

1. Have students write about a person they remember because that person changed their lives.
2. Ask students if they think they will remain friends ten years from now with the friends they have now.
3. Ask students how they want to be remembered.

LITERATURE LINKS

Grades K–4

What Is a Community From A to Z? by Bobbie Kalman (2000) will help young children see what makes up a community and how communities run. Ask students about how we all play a role in their community in a class discussion.

Grades 4–10

Mapping the World by Heart by David Smith (2003) is a must-have for every teacher. The book includes a how-to guide for teachers, lesson plans, blank maps, and game ideas. Have students create a map of their school or their town.

> **The dream begins, most of the time, with a teacher who believes in you, who tugs and pushes and leads you on to the next plateau, sometimes poking you with a sharp stick called truth.**
>
> —Dan Ruther

THIS QUOTE MAKES ME THINK ABOUT . . .

PROMPTING TEACHERS' DEEPER THINKING

- Do you believe in all of your students? What do you believe in?
- What dream do you give your students?
- Do you remember a teacher who jabbed you with the sharp stick of truth?

LESSON LINKS

1. Ask students if they can recall the teacher or teachers who tugged or pushed them to a new level.
2. Have students list the names of individuals who inspired them.
3. Ask students who helps them pursue their dreams.

LITERATURE LINKS

Grades K–4

Where Do I Live? by Neil Chesanow (1995) teaches children about where they live in terms of their house, then their street; then it keeps going to discuss the child's place in the world. Have students discuss Lesson Link #2 after reading this book.

Grades 4–10

Leaving Home: Stories by Hazel Rochman (1998) is a book for adolescents that contains stories from different writers of what they experienced when they left home to begin their adulthood. Have students describe, in stories of their own, what they think they will go through when they leave home.

Each of us is great insofar as we perceive and act on the infinite possibilities which lie undiscovered and unrecognized about us. **99**

—James Harvey Robinson

THIS QUOTE MAKES ME THINK ABOUT . . .

PROMPTING TEACHERS' DEEPER THINKING

- What do you think is the most important teaching trait you possess that others have not acknowledged?
- Do you think each of your students has infinite possibilities? Which students are the most difficult for you to see in their best light? Could they assist you in an area of classroom management? (If they did, their worth to the classroom would increase for everyone.)
- Do you perceive yourself as great? Why or why not? What action can you take to strengthen your self-perception?

LESSON LINKS

1. Ask students if they believe that they are capable of much more than they see in themselves now. Do they push themselves?
2. Ask students if they believe that they can be anything they want to be. Who can help them do this?
3. Have students write about how they perceive themselves: as great individuals, students, athletes, artists, etc.

LITERATURE LINKS

Grades K–4

Me on the Map by Joan Sweeney (1998) is an excellent book to start teaching children about how and why we use maps. Ask them where they would go if they could travel anywhere.

Grades 4–10

Necessary Noise: Stories About Our Families as They Are by Michael Cart (2003) is a collection of stories about today's families and how that term fits more than just what it used to. Let students write about Lesson Link #2 in their journals.

The very least you can do in your life is to figure out what you hope for. And the most you can do is to live inside that hope. Not admire it from a distance but live right in it, under its roof.

—Barbara Kingsolver

THIS QUOTE MAKES ME THINK ABOUT . . .

PROMPTING TEACHERS' DEEPER THINKING

- What hopes do you have for your students?
- What hopes do you have for yourself?
- What hope do you live inside, under its roof?

LESSON LINKS

1. Have students write about what hope means to them.
2. Ask students what it means to "live inside that hope."
3. Ask students what their hopes are for themselves. For their families? For their friends?

LITERATURE LINKS

Grades K–4

Mapping Penny's World by Loreen Leedy (2003) is a useful book when teaching about the features on a map—for example, what the compass rose is. Ask students what hopes they have for our planet, and have them record their answers in their journals.

Grades 4–10

It's Your World—If You Don't Like It, Change It: Activism for Teens by Mikki Halpin (2004) shows students how to act on their beliefs in regard to community problems. This book will be useful with a writing assignment on what difference a person can make in a town, a school, or a classroom. Have students discuss in groups what they would change about the world and why.

The only limit to our realization of tomorrow will be our doubts of today. Let us move forward with strong and active faith. 99

—Franklin Roosevelt

THIS QUOTE MAKES ME THINK ABOUT . . .

PROMPTING TEACHERS' DEEPER THINKING

- Can you establish a method by which you alter doubts when they enter your mind? Can you take a positive action toward situations in which you have personal doubts of success?
- What does tomorrow bring to you as a professional? Does a smile cross your face as you answer this question, indicating that you are looking forward to that day?
- What self-doubts do you have about teaching? How can you move forward tomorrow to overcome them?

LESSON LINKS

1. Have students write about the doubts they have about themselves.
2. Ask students if they have faith in themselves, and what were the most important events or people in their lives that built that faith. How can they help build the faith in themselves that others have in them?
3. Ask students what goals they share and move toward with others. Ask the class to establish a goal together, develop a plan to reach it, and establish a time in which they can evaluate how the experience increases their faith in each other. After this experience, ask the class how they can use setting goals with others as a way to increase everyone's ability to value each other.

LITERATURE LINKS

Grades K–4

My Town by Rebecca Treays (1998) will help you teach about what makes up a town. Ask students to describe what their town might be like in 5 years, in 10 years, or in 20 years.

Grades 4–10

Destiny's Gift by Natasha Anastasia Tarpley and Adioa J. Burrowes (2004) is about a girl who gets the community involved to help save her favorite bookstore from closing. Have students discuss whether faith and belief in something are the same or are different.

66 It takes a special person
With patience and wisdom to share
To unlock the treasure awaiting
Within children everywhere. 99

—Joan Zatorski

THIS QUOTE MAKES ME THINK ABOUT . . .

PROMPTING TEACHERS' DEEPER THINKING

- What does it take to be a teacher?
- Do you consider yourself a patient and wise person?
- What treasures lie within you?

LESSON LINKS

1. Ask students how they discover their potential.
2. Ask students if they believe they have treasure inside themselves.
3. Ask students if they think their teachers believe in them.

LITERATURE LINKS

Grades K–4

Any Small Goodness: A Novel of the Barrio by Tony Johnson and Raul Colon (2001) is a book about a Chicano family and how they make the best of it in a new community. This is an excellent book for when a new student comes into the room or for students at the beginning of the year.

Grades 4–10

Coming of Age in America: A Multicultural Anthology by Mary Frosch (1995) is a book of short stories about adolescence and growing up. Have students explore their talents or skills by hosting a small talent show in your classroom.

Knowledge—like the sky—is never private property . . . Teaching is the art of sharing.

—Abraham Joshua Heschel

THIS QUOTE MAKES ME THINK ABOUT . . .

PROMPTING TEACHERS' DEEPER THINKING

- Do you consider teaching an art?
- Do you share your lessons or ideas with fellow teachers? If not, how can you implement this practice schoolwide?
- Do others share their lessons with you?

LESSON LINKS

1. Ask students what sharing means to them.

2. Ask students how they share with others.

3. Have students discuss things they do that are helpful at home.

LITERATURE LINKS

Grades K–4

Jobs People Do by Christopher Maynard (2001) is a book filled with great photographs on different jobs. This is an excellent book for a child or class when discussing what professions interest them and what specific clothes are required for certain professions.

Grades 4–10

No Easy Answers: Short Stories About Teenagers Making Tough Choices by Donald R. Gallo (1999) is a book filled with stories that teenagers will be able to understand and relate to. After reading this book, have students create a song or poem about how they help out at school or at home.

CLOSING REFLECTIONS

Quotes That Inspire You to Collaborate With Your Community

A Reflection on My Personal Literacy Goals

Use this space to write a reflection on the goals you have achieved or positive actions you have taken related to literacy or reading.

My Reading Success Story

Use this space to document any of your reading success stories.

THEMED COLLECTION 11 BOOK LIST

Cart, M. (2003). *Necessary Noise: Stories About Our Families as They Are.* New York: HarperTempest

Caseley, J. (2002). *On the Town: A Community Adventure.* New York: HarperCollins.

Chesanow, N. (1995). *Where Do I Live?* Hauppauge, New York: Barron's Educational Series.

Frosch, M. (1995). *Coming of Age in America: A Multicultural Anthology.* New York: The New Press.

Gallo, D. (1999). *No Easy Answers: Short Stories About Teenagers Making Tough Choices.* New York: Random House.

Halpin, M. (2004). *It's Your World—If You Don't Like It, Change It: Activism for Teenagers.* New York: Simon & Schuster.

Johnson, T., & Colon, R. (2001). *Any Small Goodness: A Novel of the Barrio.* New York: Scholastic.

Kalman, B. (2000). *What Is a Community From A to Z?* New York: Crabtree.

Leedy, L. (2003). *Mapping Penny's World.* New York: Henry Holt.

Maynard, C. (2001). *Jobs People Do.* New York: DK Children.

Menzel, P., Mann, C., & Kennedy, P. (1995). *Material World: A Global Family Portrait.* San Francisco: Sierra Club Books.

Pollak, B. (2004). *Our Community Garden.* Hillsboro, OR: Beyond Words.

Rochman, H. (1998). *Leaving Home: Stories.* New York: HarperTrophy.

Rondeau, A. (2004). *Do Something in Your Community.* Edina, MN: ABDO.

Smith, D. (2002). *If the World Were a Village: A Book About the World's People.* Toronto, ON: Kids Can Press.

Smith, D. (2003). *Mapping the World by Heart.* New York: Scholastic.

Solheim, J. (2001). *It's Disgusting and We Ate It! True Food Facts From Around the World and Throughout History.* New York: Simon & Schuster.

Sweeney, J. (1998). *Me on the Map.* New York: Random House.

Tarpley, N., & Burrowes, A. (2004). *Destiny's Gift.* New York: Lee & Low Books.

Treays, R. (1998). *My Town.* Tulsa, OK: Educational Development Corporation.

Favorite Additional Quotes From Teachers and Students

Susan E. Israel

These quotations are provided so that you can use this book for many years. We wanted you to have the opportunity to substitute any of the following quotes for a quote that appeared in a chapter that does not meet your students' needs.

We also developed this list so that you could select any quote from the following pages to add to a quote that we have developed Lesson Links and Literature Selections to match. For example, you may want to place a quote from this book on the board and follow it with a quote that states the same message in a slightly different fashion. If you select this method of using the following quotes, students could discuss such topics as:

- How does a choice of words change the emphasis in meaning in a quotation?
- How can the same idea be expressed in two different ways?
- Why does one quotation mean more to the students than another?

If you decide to use a quote from the chapters of this book and a quote from the list below on the same day, you can choose a quote below with a different objective in mind. The quote you choose could communicate a value that is the exact opposite or extremely different from the other with which you pair it. If you select this method of using the following quotes, students could discuss these questions:

- When two values contradict, how do you select which path to follow?
- How can two dissimilar morals or values coexist in the same culture?
- Do you think that values in a society change so that when a quotation is created it could serve as truth for people living at that time but it would lose its value for people who live in a different period of time?

A third reason that we created the list that follows is that we wanted you to have enough quotations for daily use for a full school year. We have provided over 100 quotations in this book without this list. Thus, the following quotes can be used for the remaining days in the school year.

THEMED COLLECTION 1: MAKING MEANINGFUL CONNECTIONS

Teaching should be such that what is offered is perceived as a valuable gift.

—Albert Einstein

A teacher's purpose is not to create students in his own image, but to develop students who can create their own image.

—Author Unknown

In youth we learn: In age we understand.

—Marie Von Ebner-Eschenbach

Throw your dreams into space like a kite, and you do not know what it will bring back: a new life, a new friend, a new love, a new country.

—Anais Nin

Grab a chance and you won't be sorry for what might have been.

—Arthur Ransome

When you are kind to someone in trouble, you hope they'll remember and be kind to someone else. And it'll become like a wildfire.

—Whoopi Goldberg

Accept the challenges, so that you may feel the exhilaration of victory.

—George S. Patton

Failure is success if we learn from it.

—Malcolm S. Forbes

Well done is better than well said.

—Ben Franklin

Everyone who remembers his own educational experiences remembers teachers, not methods and techniques. The teacher is the kingpin of the educational situation. He makes or breaks programs.

—Sidney Hook

THEMED COLLECTION 2: SETTING VALUABLE GOALS

You must be the change you wish to see in the world.

—Mahatma Gandhi

If you have built castles in the sky, your work need not be lost; that is where they should be. Now put foundations under them.

—Henry David Thoreau

All things are possible until they are proved impossible—even the impossible may only be so as of now.

—Pearl S. Buck

Make it a rule of life never to regret and never to look back. We all live in suspense, from day to day, from hour to hour; in other words, we are the hero of our own story.

—Mary McCarthy

It's never too late to be what you might have been.

—George Eliot

There are two mistakes one can make along the road to truth—not going all the way, and not starting.

—Siddhartha Gautama Buddha

Yesterday is history, tomorrow is a mystery, and today is a gift; that's why they call it the present.

—Eleanor Roosevelt

Education would be much more effective if its purpose was to ensure that by the time they leave school every boy and girl should know how much they do not know, and be imbued with a lifelong desire to know it.

—Sir William Haley

THEMED COLLECTION 3: USING ASSESSMENT TO EXCEL

You can have anything you want if you want it desperately enough. You must want it with an inner exuberance that erupts through the skin and joins the energy that created the world.

—Sheila Graham

And the day came when the risk to remain in a tight bud was more painful than the risk it took to blossom.

—Anais Nin

Failure is impossible.

—Susan B. Anthony

The most wasted of all days is one without laughter.

—e. e. cummings

THEMED COLLECTION 4: BUILDING BLOCKS FOR SUCCESS

Congratulations! Today is your day. You're off to great places. You're off and away!... And will you succeed? Yes, you will indeed! (98 and ¾% guaranteed.) Kid, you'll move mountains!

—Dr. Seuss

The highest result of education is tolerance.

—Helen Keller

Children learn through all their senses, to develop a sense for order and logical thought.

—Maria Montessori

Good teaching is one-fourth preparation and three-fourths pure theatre.

—Gail Godwin

We are all worms, but I do believe I'm a glowworm.

—Sir Winston Churchill

Never bend your head; always hold it high. Look the world in the face.

—Helen Keller

THEMED COLLECTION 5: WORD POWER EQUALS KNOWLEDGE

All good literature is a treasure of honey in the combs of God.

—C. V. Devan Nair

Imagination is more important than knowledge.

—Albert Einstein

THEMED COLLECTION 6:
EXPANDING OUR OPPORTUNITY

There's much to be said for challenging fate instead of ducking behind it.

—Diana Trilling

I am where I am because I believe in all possibilities.

—Whoopi Goldberg

Do not go where the path may lead. Go instead where there is no path and leave a trail.

—Ralph Waldo Emerson

The purpose of learning is growth, and our minds, unlike our bodies, can continue growing as we continue to live.

—Mortimer Adler

The process of scientific discovery is, in effect, a continual flight from wonder.

—Albert Einstein

Surely whoever speaks to me in the right voice, him or her I shall follow.

—Walt Whitman

THEMED COLLECTION 7:
THINKING TO OBTAIN MEANING

Miracles are instantaneous; they cannot be summoned but they come of themselves, usually at unlikely moments and to those who least expect them.

—Katherine A. Porter

Curiosity has its own reason for existing. Never lose a holy curiosity.

—Albert Einstein

Good teaching is more asking of right questions than giving of right answers.

—Josef Albers

It must be remembered that the purpose of education is not to fill the minds of students with facts. It is to teach them to think, if that is possible, and always to think for themselves.

—Robert Hutchins

There is nothing like a little experience to upset a theory and improve a theory.

—Author Unknown

THEMED COLLECTION 8: IDENTIFYING OUR STRENGTHS

I've found the worry and irritation vanish into thin air the moment I open my mind to the many blessings I possess.

—Dale Carnegie

I will tell you what I have learned for myself. For me a long, five- or six-mile walk helps. And one must go alone and every day.

—Brenda Ueland

The job of an educator is to teach students to see the vitality in themselves.

—Joseph Campbell

Keep your sense of humor. There's enough stress in the rest of your life to let bad shots ruin a game you're supposed to enjoy.

—Amy Strum Alcott

Let it not be lost on one that one of the most important jobs in this country is teaching. Teachers can influence and motivate an entire generation.

—Abigail Van Buren

A person may make mistakes, but isn't a failure until he (or she) starts blaming someone else. We must believe in ourselves, and somewhere along the road of life, we must meet someone who sees greatness in us, expects it from us, and lets us know it. It is the golden key to success.

—Ann Landers

THEMED COLLECTION 9: WORK, STUDY SKILLS, AND WRITING

I am only one. But still I am one. I cannot do everything, but still I can do something. I will not refuse to do the something I can do.

—Helen Keller

The past cannot be changed. The future is yet in your power.

—Mary Pickford

You don't have to plan to fail, all you have to do is fail to plan.

—Author Unknown

I can be flexible.

—Author Unknown

THEMED COLLECTION 10: LITERACY WORLDS

Readers are leaders. Thinkers succeed.

—Marva Collins

Become a person who neither looks up to the rich or down on the poor . . . take your share of the world and let other people have theirs.

—George Washington Carver

I know no safe depository of the ultimate powers of society but the people themselves.

—Thomas Jefferson

THEMED COLLECTION 11: COLLABORATIVE COMMUNITIES AT SCHOOL AND HOME

Teaching is not just a job. It is a human service, and it must be thought of as a mission.

—Dr. Ralph Tyler

A rejected opportunity to give is a lost opportunity to receive.

—William Arthur Ward

To live for a time close to great minds is the best kind of education.

—John Buchan

Quotation Bibliography

Quotes in this book came from the sources shown below as well as from the authors' personal collections.

Backes, L. (2001). *Best books for kids who think they hate to read: 125 books that will turn any child into a lifelong reader.* New York: Prima.

Block, C. C. (1998). *Quotes: Book 1, 2, 3.* Unpublished manuscripts, Texas Christian University School of Education, Fort Worth.

Great quotes from great teachers. (1996). Glendale Heights, IL: Great Quotations Publishing.

Teacher's inspirations: Motivational quotes for you and your students. (1990). Glendale Heights, IL: Great Quotations Publishing.

The Educators Network: http://www.theeducatorsnetwork.com/quotes/

Daily Celebrations, Quotations Directory: http://www.dailycelebrations.com/quotes.htm

Quotes for Teachers: www.motivateus.com/teachers.htm

Yopp, R. H., & Yopp, H. K. (2001). *Literature-based reading activities* (3rd ed.) Boston: Allyn and Bacon.

Index

**CORWIN
PRESS**

The Corwin Press logo—a raven striding across an open book—represents the union of courage and learning. Corwin Press is committed to improving education for all learners by publishing books and other professional development resources for those serving the field of PreK–12 education. By providing practical, hands-on materials, Corwin Press continues to carry out the promise of its motto: **"Helping Educators Do Their Work Better."**